Readers Praise Patricia Evans's
The Verbally Abusive Relationship

"This is the first time I have read a book about myself. It is so clearly defined—I believe this book has saved my life."
J.M., Danville, New Hampshire

"I have highlighted practically the whole book . . . I recommended it to my youngest daughter just an hour ago. Wish I'd been able to read it 36 years ago!"
M.M., Sedalia, Missouri

"No one has ever explained this tragedy as you have."
A.W., Denver, Colorado

"Thank you for writing (this book) for me and the thousands of women everywhere who suffer in abusive relationships."
B.L., Clayton, California

"I had to steal the eight dollars to buy this book because he would not allow it . . . I thought verbal abuse just consisted of name-calling. Boy, was I wrong."
L.H., Douglassville, Pennsylvania

"I can't tell you how refreshing it is to finally read a book on this subject . . . Reading your book has confirmed everything I have been feeling."
J.M., Pittsburgh, Pennsylvania

"An invaluable contribution to helping us understand and cope with our relationship problems."
B.R., Washington, D.C.

"Your book *The Verbally Abusive Relationship* has saved my life emotionally and, probably, physically, as I was at a point of wanting to die . . . Thank you for your time, for my life."
J.F., Redondo Beach, California

"I couldn't believe what I saw on your pages. I thank God every day for the work you have done."
A.W., Spokane, Washington

THE VERBALLY ABUSIVE RELATIONSHIP

How to recognize it and how to respond

EXPANDED SECOND EDITION

Patricia Evans

ADAMS MEDIA CORPORATION
Avon, Massachusetts

Published by Adams Media, an F+W Publications Company
57 Littlefield Street, Avon, MA 02322. U.S.A.

ISBN 13: 978-1-55850-582-7
ISBN 10: 1-55850-582-2

Printed in Canada.

T S R Q P O

Library of Congress Cataloging-in-Publication Data
Evans, Patricia (Patricia)
The verbally abusive relationship : how to recognize it and how to respond /
Patricia Evans. — Expanded 2nd. ed.
p.   cm.
Includes bibliographical references and index.
ISBN 1-55850-582-2 (pbk.)
1. Interpersonal conflict—United States. 2. Family violence—United States.
3. Invective—United States. 4. Psychological abuse—United States. 5. Control
(Psychology)—United States. 6. Influence (Psychology)—United States.
7. Wife abuse—United States—Psychological aspects. I. Title.
BF637.I48E92   1996
362.82'92—dc20   96-993
CIP

This publication is designed to provide accurate and authoritative information with regard to the subject matter covered. It is sold with the understanding that the publisher is
not engaged in rendering legal, accounting, or other professional advice. If legal advice
or other expert assistance is required, the services of a qualified professional person
should be sought.
— From a *Declaration of Principles* jointly adopted by a Committee of the American Bar
Association and a Committee of Publishers and Associations

This book is available at quantity discounts for bulk purchases.
For information, call 1-800-289-0963.

Visit our home page at http://www.adamsmedia.com

Acknowledgments

I am grateful to all who supported me in writing this book. Especially, I wish to acknowledge the many women who so courageously shared their stories and their insights with me.

While I wrote and rewrote, I had constant encouragement from my sister, Beverly Amori. She never for a moment let me harbor any doubts about the value of this work. Robert Brownbridge, L.C.S.W., brought me clarity and taught me to trust myself.

The book's theme originated with a suggestion from Carl Putz, Ph.D.: "If you could only tell people how to recognize verbal abuse, that would be something!" I thank Carl, not only for suggesting the theme of recognition, but also for having given me the realization that I could write.

I am grateful to Patricia Seereiter, who contributed her quiet strength, her lively spirit, and the serenity of her studio "oasis"—a perfect place to write.

Pat Corrington, L.C.S.W., cheered me with her wonderful enthusiasm and provided her editing skills as well. She has a special place in my heart. Susan Hiraki, M.F.C.C., most graciously gave me encouragement and insightful commentary.

I thank Kate Gann for her interesting contributions and Donna and friends for their unfailing emotional support.

Central to making this edition a reality are the following people, to whom I am most grateful: Helen McGrath, my agent, a constant source of encouragement—always ready to help; Ed Walters, my editor, a joy to work with; narrative therapist Linda Crawford of San Diego, my resource and guide into the world of narrative therapy; Craig Smith, Ph.D., Richard Maisel, Ph.D., and their colleagues, who welcomed me to their conferences. Thanks to all.

Finally, I am especially grateful to my children for their continuing confidence in me.

— *Patricia Evans*

Table of Contents

PART I

PART II

Foreword

In 1992, when this book was released, it became the first book to define and describe verbally abusive relationships between adults. At that time, I never imagined that thousands of people would respond. I deeply appreciate all the contributions and continue to learn from women's and men's perspectives and experiences.

Although the companion to this book, *Verbal Abuse Survivors Speak Out*, expands upon this topic and answers many questions, there are some additional issues that I feel need to be addressed. I am glad to have the opportunity to present them here in this new edition.

Almost all who write to me are women (over 98 percent), but some men have come forward. They are on the side of change. I find them open to learning from women's experiences. They seem to know that those who have been oppressed—those who have suffered the pain of this kind of betrayal—are best qualified to reveal the form this oppression takes and are best able to inform others of its effects.

Even though most verbally abusive relationships do *not* become violent, a good number do. Verbal abuse precedes the first incident of violence and is an ongoing part of a battering relationship. There is no doubt about this. For instance, a man does not move in with a woman and then start beating her before first disparaging her, withholding his feelings from her, or belittling her. Understanding the dynamics of these relationships and offering treatment for the abuser can be a first step toward reducing violence in the world.

Even after taking into consideration the fact that men seem more reluctant than women to reveal their experiences, it seems that verbal abuse—like battering—in adult-couple relationships is clearly a gender issue.

There are many ways that this gender difference has developed over many centuries. One very general and obvious influence is that many more men than women have been invited in numerous ways to believe that dominating another adult in a relationship is acceptable behavior. The assumption of a "right" to dominance is one of the most destructive of all assumptions. Certainly, both verbal abuse and battering take place within this context.

On the other hand, few women have been invited by cultural messages to dominate their mate. Either way, the attitude that domination is acceptable is nonsense. People are meant to be in charge of themselves—self-responsible; and from childhood to adulthood they are meant to develop their ability to be inner-directed—true to themselves, not subject to another person.

Attitudes are continuing to change through the efforts of men and women who realize that verbal abuse not only harms the partner but also the family and ultimately our society as a whole.

There is evidence that, as a culture, we are becoming increasingly intolerant of abuse. Just a generation ago, harassment and battering were not even recognized as acts to be prosecuted in the courts. Why? Because they were assaults against women.

I am always shocked to find that some people even teach oppression—the idea that one adult should obey another adult in an adult relationship. The forces of ignorance master the minds of many, who then, without even realizing it, perpetuate abuse. Of course, each one of us may see the problem differently and may give it a different name. One name for the problem is "patriarchy."

Beyond expressing these thoughts, I have added three new chapters to this new edition that I think you will find useful.

"About Therapy—And for the Therapist" discusses therapy and patriarchy. It is intended to support therapists and *all* readers who deal with verbal abuse issues.

"Children and Verbal Abuse" addresses the concerns of part-time parents who need to keep their lives and activities separate from a former spouse, and at the same time want their child (or children) raised in a nurturing environment.

The last chapter, "Frequently Asked Questions," answers some questions that are not already addressed in *Verbal Abuse Survivors Speak Out.*

I find that there is much love and goodness in the world. I believe also that much of the pain we find in the world is only there to remind us that something is wrong. It's time to find out what it is. I hope this new edition serves you.

Preface

I believe that we are in the midst of an evolution—an evolution in consciousness. This evolution is manifested by the increasing value we attribute to the individual human being and by our increasing interest in our human potentiality.

As we have come to understand our human rights, we have grown in our respect for human life and human dignity. We have seen old power structures and old beliefs disintegrate in the light of higher consciousness. Collectively, we no longer condone slavery, child labor, child abuse, or wife battering. Collectively, we are crossing a threshold from a belief in Power Over (dominance) to a belief in Personal Power (mutuality and co-creation).

This is a long and arduous crossing, and the progress we witness seems small in relation to the problems still with us. As we cross this threshold we give up Power Over and gain conscious awareness of our Personal Power. An example of this crossing is the new freedom of the people of Russia—a turning point in world history.

We are aware of politically and economically repressive systems that are maintained by physical force. We are less aware of psychological repression. This repression is maintained by verbal manipulation and coercion. I believe, therefore, that even as we act to advance the cause of physical freedom at many levels and in many arenas, we may also act to recognize and free ourselves from this less obvious, yet all too pervasive, form of control. Repressive systems perpetuate themselves as long as they remain unrecognized.

Introduction

This book is for everyone. It happens that the examples, experiences, and stories it contains were told to me by women. Consequently, and hopefully without prejudice, I refer to the feminine experience of the confusion and pain of verbal abuse. In order to protect the confidentiality of the women who shared their experiences with me, I have changed their names and the identifying circumstances. The women I describe are composites. They are the partners or former partners of verbal abusers.

Verbal abuse is a kind of battering which doesn't leave evidence comparable to the bruises of physical battering. It can be just as painful, and recovery can take much longer. The victim of abuse lives in a gradually more confusing realm. In public she is with one man, in private he may become another. Subtle diminishing or angry outbursts, cool indifference or one-upmanship, witty sarcasm or silent withholding, manipulative coercion or unreasonable demands are common occurrences. They are, however, cloaked in a "what's wrong with you, making a big thing out of nothing" attitude, and many, many other forms of denial. Often, for the verbally abused woman, there is *no* other witness to her reality, and no one who can understand her experience. Friends and family may see the abuser as a really nice guy and, certainly, he sees himself as one.

Although this book describes women's experiences, it is a fact that some men suffer verbal abuse from their mates. Generally, however, they do not live in the kind of fear women experience with an angry man.

If you have been verbally abused, you have been told in subtle and not-so-subtle ways that your perception of reality is wrong and that your feelings are wrong. Consequently, you may doubt your own experience and, at the same time, not realize that you are doing so. I suggest that, as you read about the experience of verbal abuse, you notice if this kind of experience seems familiar to you.

This book is designed to enable you to recognize subtle verbal abuse and manipulation. My intention is to reveal the nuances and reality of verbal abuse as experienced by the partners of the verbal abusers. All would be pleased to forget the past, never recalling the painful events which led to the writing of a book such as this. We would all like to forget the problems of our collective past. We can, however, learn from the past and through informed awareness make conscious choices which insure a better future. Any one person's disparagement diminishes us all.

The Verbally Abusive Relationship is based upon my interviews with 40 verbally abused women. Their ages ranged from 21 to 66. The average length of their relationship was a little over 16 years. Collectively, therefore, I have drawn upon more than 640 years of experience with verbal abuse. Most of the women I interviewed had left a verbally abusive relationship. Recognition and integration of what had occurred was still going on, five, ten, and fifteen years later. Many had tried every avenue, every approach, to improve their relationship: explaining, overlooking, asking, begging, individual and joint counseling, living their lives as independently as possible, meeting their own needs, not asking "too much," settling for less and less, being undemanding, being understanding. Nothing seemed to work. The dynamics of the relationship were often still a mystery.

If, after reading this book, you suspect that you are in a verbally abusive relationship, I hope that you will seek professional counseling—and will bring this book with you. You will need support and the validation of your reality. There are possibilities for a happy relationship if *both* parties are willing to change.

A Very Important Word of Caution

If you have been the victim of verbal abuse, if you have searched your soul for answers to the questions of how you can say things so he will understand, how it is that you hear what he says he never said, or how it is that you feel what he says you shouldn't feel, you may have been led to believe that there is something basically wrong with your ability to communicate, or with your perceptions or feelings. You may now be asking, "How can I change my basic nature? After all, didn't I just read, 'There are possibilities for a happy relationship if both parties are willing to change'?"

Don't despair. I do not suggest that, in order to determine if you can have a happy relationship with your mate, you change your nature, instead I suggest that when you recognize what you are encountering, you respond to what you are recognizing in a specific way—a way that requests change. By doing so, you may encounter your fear of "loss of love." By not doing so, you may encounter your fear of "loss of self."

The underlying premise of this book is that verbal abuse is an issue of control, a means of holding power over another. This abuse may be overt or covert, constant, controlling, and what Bach and Deutsch (1980) call "crazymaking."

The effects of verbal abuse are primarily qualitative. That is, they cannot be seen like the effects of physical abuse. There are no physical signs of injury, no bruises, black eyes, or broken bones. The intensity of anguish which the victim suffers determines the extent of the injury. The quality of the experience of the victim defines the degree of abuse.

My primary purpose is to enable you, the reader, to recognize verbal abuse. Since verbal abuse is experiential in nature, this book, as a whole, is about experience.

Significant facts which add perspective to the material in this book are these:

1. Generally, in a verbally abusive relationship the abuser denies the abuse.

2. Verbal abuse most often takes place behind closed doors.

3. Physical abuse is always preceded by verbal abuse.

The book is divided into two parts. Part I begins with a self-evaluative questionnaire. Then, from a broad perspective, it describes Power Over as a kind of power manifested by dominance and control, in contrast to Personal Power, which is manifested by mutuality and co-creation. Next, the experience, feelings, and thinking of the partner of the verbal abuser are explored. Finally, the primary patterns of abuse are described.

Part II defines the categories of verbal abuse, such as withholding, countering, discounting, and trivializing, and describes the cultural context in which the partner evaluates her experience. Appropriate methods of communicating and seeking change are explained. We then explore the underlying dynamics of the verbally abusive relationship, therapy, and children and verbal abuse. The final chapter discusses the underlying dynamics of the verbally abusive relationship.

PART I

Part I begins with an evaluation and checklist to help the reader discover unrecognized episodes of verbal abuse. Two kinds of power are described and contrasted: Power Over and Personal Power. Then, in the context of these two kinds of power, abusive and nonabusive relationships are compared. We will then explore some of the partners' experiences and discover how the verbal abuser and the partner seem to be in different realities and unable to recognize each other's worlds. We will learn how verbal abuse affects the partner—how she thinks and feels, and what she believes.

The confusion generated by both cultural conditioning and verbal abuse is discussed. Finally, patterns of abuse are described as well as the actual dreams, physical symptoms, and inner images that alerted some partners to the fact that their relationships were, in truth, not all that they had seemed to be.

CHAPTER I

Evaluating Your Own Experience

Yelling at living things does tend to kill the spirit in them. Sticks and stones may break our bones, but words will break our hearts . . . .
— *Robert Fulghum*

Most of us are aware that name calling is verbally abusive. If you have been called *idiot, dummy, bitch,* or any other derogatory name, you have been verbally abused. Name calling is the most obvious form of verbal abuse and is not difficult to recognize. Other forms of verbal abuse are less evident. Recognizing these forms of abuse in adult-couple relationships can be very difficult for many reasons. Some primary reasons follow:

1. Mostly, verbal abuse is secretive. Usually only the partner of the abuser hears it.

2. Verbal abuse becomes more intense over time. The partner becomes used to and adapted to it.

3. Verbal abuse takes many forms and disguises.

4. Verbal abuse consistently discounts the partner's perception of the abuse.

Verbal abuse is, in a sense, built into our culture. One-upmanship, defeating, putting down, topping, countering, manipulating, criticizing, hard selling, and intimidating are accepted as fair games by many. When these power plays are enacted in a relationship and denied by the perpetrator, confusion results.

The following evaluation is designed to help you determine if you are experiencing verbal abuse in a relationship. Place a check next to the statements which are true for your relationship:

❑ 1. He seems irritated or angry with you several times a week or more although you hadn't meant to upset him. You are surprised each time. (He says he's not mad when you ask him what he's mad about, or he tells you in some way that it's your fault.)

❑ 2. When you feel hurt and try to discuss your upset feelings with him, you don't feel as if the issue has been fully resolved, so you don't feel happy and relieved, nor do you have a feeling that you've "kissed and made up." (He says, "You're just trying to start an argument!" or in some other way expresses his refusal to discuss the situation.)

❑ 3. You frequently feel perplexed and frustrated by his responses because you can't get him to understand your intentions.

❑ 4. You are upset not so much about concrete issues—how much time to spend with each other, where to go on vacation, etc.—as about the communication in the relationship: what he thinks you said and what you heard him say.

❑ 5. You sometimes wonder, "What's wrong with me? I shouldn't feel so bad."

❑ 6. He rarely, if ever, seems to want to share his thoughts or plans with you.

❑ 7. He seems to take the opposite view from you on almost everything you mention, and his view is not qualified by "I think" or "I believe" or "I feel"—as if your view were wrong and his were right.

❑ 8. You sometimes wonder if he perceives you as a separate person.

❑ 9. You can't recall saying to him, "Cut it out!" or, "Stop it!"

❑ 10. He is either angry or has "no idea of what you're talking about" when you try to discuss an issue with him.

If you have agreed with two or more of these statements, this book will support you in recognizing verbal abuse. If you have not had these experiences, this book will support your empathetic understanding of those who have. If you think you've had some of these experiences, but aren't sure, read on.

Verbal abuse may be overt, such as an angry outburst directed at the partner or an attack along the lines of, "You're too sensitive." Or it may be covert, hidden, as in the case of "I don't know what you're talking about," when in fact the abuser does know.

Covert verbal abuse is subversive because of its indirect quality. It is a covert attack or coercion. This kind of abuse has been described as "crazymaking." It is "a form of interpersonal interaction that results from the repression of intense aggression and which seriously impairs its victim's capacity to recognize and deal with the interpersonal reality." (Bach and Goldberg, 1974, p. 251)

When this kind of abuse occurs, the partner has nothing specific to deal with. She must trust her own experience and, as painful as it is, come to terms with the knowledge that the abuser is not loving, valuing, and respecting her.

George R. Bach and Ronald M. Deutsch, in their book *Stop! You're Driving Me Crazy* (1980, pp. 272–273), state:

Of value in teaching recognition of the crazymaking experience is the following checklist:

1. Feeling temporarily thrown off balance and momentarily unable to right oneself.

2. Feeling lost, not knowing where to turn, searching aimlessly.

3. Being caught off guard.

4. Feeling disconnected, confused, disoriented.

5. Feeling off balance, as if the rug had been pulled from under one's feet.

6. Receiving double messages but somehow unable or fearful to ask for clarification. [Author's note: Or asking for clarification but not getting it.]

7. Feeling generally "bugged" by the simple presence of a person.

8. To discover that one was mistaken in one's evaluation of where one stood or what it was all about.

9. Feeling totally unprepared for a broken promise or unfulfilled expectation.

10. Experiencing the shattering of an important "dream."

11. Where one assumed goodwill, ill will *seems* to prevail.

12. One feels pushed around, not in control of one's own direction.

13. Unable to get off redundantly spinning circles of thoughts.

14. What seemed clear becomes muddled.

15. An uneasy, weird feeling of emptiness.

16. A strong wish to get away, yet feeling unable to move, as if frozen.

17. One is befuddled, not able to attack the problem.

18. Feeling vaguely suspicious that something is wrong.

19. Feeling that one's subjective world has become chaotic.

[Reprinted by the permission of Putnam Publishing Group, NY, from *Stop! You're Driving Me Crazy* by Dr. George R. Bach and Ronald M. Deutsch, copyright 1980 by Dr. George R. Bach and Ronald M. Deutsch.]

You may recognize some of the feelings and experiences described above. Others may not be clear to you. Some partners of verbal abusers recognize, after being away from the relationship for a while, that they "used to feel that way."

Verbal abuse is hostile aggression. The abuser is not provoked by his mate. The abuser may consciously or even unconsciously deny what he is doing. In any case, he is not likely to wake up one day and say, "Oh, my! Look what I've been doing. I'm really sorry. I won't do it any more." No one but the partner experiences it. Usually, only the partner can recognize it. "The aggression can be recognized because the impact of the behavior on the victim is a hurtful one." (Bach and Goldberg, 1974, p. 119)

Generally the responsibility for recognizing verbal abuse rests with the partner of the abuser, because the abuser is not motivated to change. However, the partner may have difficulty recognizing the abuse for what it is because she is led to doubt her feelings. For example, if she feels hurt or upset by something her mate has said and she expresses her feeling, saying, "I felt bad when you said that," the verbal abuser, instead of recognizing her feeling and responding appropriately, will reject and invalidate her feeling by saying something like, "I don't know what you're talking about. You're too sensitive." The partner then doubts her own perception. Why? In childhood, like many, she may have been taught that her feelings were to be ignored. Feelings, however, are essential to our being, because they are the criteria by which we determine if something is wrong or unsafe.

When the partner can recognize and validate her feelings, she can begin to recognize verbal abuse. In other words, she might say:

I feel hurt, I am being hurt.

I feel diminished, I am being diminished.

I feel unrecognized, I am being unrecognized.

I feel ignored, I am being ignored.

I feel made fun of, I am being made fun of.

I feel discounted, I am being discounted.

I feel closed off, I am being closed off.

(You may fill in the next one, and so on.)

I feel _____ , I am being _____.

If the partner shares her feelings with the perpetrator of the aggression, *you can be absolutely certain, he will invalidate them.* He may, for example, deride her with a sarcastic comment and then, when she protests, tell her it was a joke. The partner may then doubt the truth of her own perceptions. However, "the very impression of truth is likely to be perceived, not from another's vision, but from one's own." (Bach and Deutsch, 1980, p. 207)

CHAPTER II

Two Kinds of Power: A Broad Perspective

The world without spirit is a wasteland.
— *Joseph Campbell*

There are two kinds of power. One kills the spirit. The other nourishes the spirit. The first is Power Over. The other is Personal Power.

Power Over shows up as control and dominance. Personal Power shows up as mutuality and co-creation. Mutuality is a way of being with another person which promotes the growth and well-being of one's self *and* the other person by means of clear communication and empathetic understanding. Co-creation is a consciously shared participation in life which helps one reach one's goals. (These ideas will be discussed more fully in Chapters III and IV.)

Since verbal abuse is symptomatic of personal, cultural, and global problems which originate with the misuse of power, I shall begin with a broad perspective and a comprehensive look at Power Over.

Power Over is one model of how the world is believed to work. A belief in Power Over resembles a lens through which the believer views the world. Someone who believes in Power Over expects to get what he or she wants through the use of Power Over another. Our Western civilization was founded on Power Over. Now as a civilization, we have tremendous Power Over the earth and its peoples and resources. We have the power to wipe out our world. We have the power of total destruction. The Power Over model is, I believe, no longer tenable. Some of the symptoms of living and acting through this paradigm are pollution, potential global anni-hilation, hunger and homelessness, prejudice and tyranny.

These concerns bring into sharp focus our regard for human dignity and the quality of life. The Power Over paradigm holds Power Over life. Power Over life may deny the value and quality of life. The Power Over model of control and dominance has per-meated individual consciousness for thousands of years and has taken us to the brink of global chaos.

Our science shows us that out of chaos new order arises. Where will the new order come from? It cannot be legislated, nor can it be established through more wars and more Power Over. I believe this new order can arise only out of individual conscious-ness. For this reason, the recognition of verbal abuse as a means of controlling, dominating, and having Power Over another person is of real concern to us all.

Since the microcosm of personal relationship influences the macrocosm of civilization just as the civilization—its customs and culture—influences personal relationship, it is in our relationships that we might effect this change. If so, an opportunity is present today in our everyday lives. It is the opportunity we have to value ourselves and to awaken to the way we *express and protect* that value in our relationships.

If we are to recognize and free ourselves from the influence of the Power Over model, we must hear ourselves—what words we speak and in what manner we speak them. Likewise, we must hear the words spoken to us and the manner in which they are spoken. This awareness can bring us to the realization of how we do or do not dignify, respect, protect, and esteem ourselves and ul-timately all life. We can begin by having faith in our own value and by trusting our own perceptions.

This may be very difficult for the partner of a verbal abuser because verbal abuse creates victims just as any other subversive system does. Verbal abuse by its very nature undermines and dis-counts its victim's perceptions. Few of the women I interviewed were aware of what was happening in their relationship; certainly they did not see themselves as victims. They just knew something was wrong. If one of them had left her relationship, very often her reasons for leaving involved other issues.

In a verbally abusive relationship, the partner learns to toler-ate abuse without realizing it and to lose self-esteem without real-izing it. She is blamed by the abuser and becomes the scapegoat. The partner is then the victim.

Interestingly, in Christian thought, Christ was the *last* victim and the *last* scapegoat. He died for all humanity. This message seems to have been obscured by the prevailing worldview of Power Over and "might makes right," which also, of course, makes victims and scapegoats.

As we will see, the victims of verbal abuse must wrest a sense of their own value and their self-esteem from the most disempowering and confusing of circumstances. They can do so by recognizing verbal abuse for what it is.

What is the origin of the Power Over model? It is the result of, and the perpetuator of, "poisonous pedagogy" discussed in Alice Miller's book *For Your Own Good* and in John Bradshaw's works. A poisonous pedagogy is a toxic method of teaching or raising a child. It is a method which controls the behavior of the child by the misuse of Power Over the child. This misuse of power causes the child extreme pain. If the child becomes an adult without having worked through the hurt and pain of the experience, he will perpetuate the misuse of power in adulthood. Consequently, the adult can become toxic or poisonous to others. This toxicity is what we find in abusive relationships.

We have looked at the Power Over model and at the fact that individuals as well as nations are motivated to control and dominate others. We may note that *their illusion of power is maintained only as long as they have an "other" to have power over.* Tragically, many are desperate to maintain this stance, because it is the only power they know. If there is no "other," one is created.

Personal Power is another way of experiencing power, one which doesn't need winners and losers, dominant people and subordinates, and which doesn't require Power Over an "other." Personal Power works by mutuality and co-creation and may be considered a new way of being in and perceiving the world.

Let us explore these ideas in the context of a relationship, for here is where we often find two people living and perceiving through the two different models; one is living by Power Over, the other in Personal Power. Through these lenses these two people may see neither each other nor each other's reality.

As I researched verbally abusive relationships, the most significant and surprising discovery I made was that *the verbal abuser and the partner seemed to be living in two different realities.* The abuser's orientation was toward control and dominance. The partner's orientation was toward mutuality and co-creation. In many respects they *were* in two different realities.

In order to understand them better, let us assume that they do live in separate realities and, for simplicity, let us call these realities Reality I and Reality II. Reality I and Reality II correspond to the Power Over and Personal Power models. In other words, *those who feel power through dominance and control (Power Over) are living in Reality I. Those who feel power through mutuality and creativity (Personal Power) are living in Reality II.*

It seems that we live in a world that cannot yet accept Reality II while the dangers of remaining in Reality I become more evident. Unable to begin thinking according to the new model, we live under the threat of annihilation, seemingly caught between conflicting realities.

We can move out of this conflict and struggle by understanding what happens when people from these two realities form a relationship and if we are in Reality II, becoming adept at recognizing people who are in Reality I. For example, "All is fair in love and war" is a Reality I perception. Below is an example of what may happen in a relationship when each person is in a different reality.

If the partner of the abuser grew up under the influence of Reality I and then emerged in Reality II, she may find it extremely difficult to distinguish between the two realities. She may be living in Reality II and seeking mutuality without having achieved Reality II self-esteem—rather like a fish out of water, not yet an amphibian.

A significant fact I discovered was that many women living in Reality II accepted and responded to communications from Reality I as if the communications were valid. The following example shows how that can happen. (It may be worthwhile to read this example a couple of times because it illustrates a core problem in abusive relationships.)

Ann is in Reality II (RII), and she believes that Zee is in RII with her. We know that he isn't. As you follow their conversation, you will see how Ann slips for a moment into a place between RII, where she lives, and Reality I (RI) where Zee lives. Also, you will see how Ann assumes all along that Zee is in *her* reality.

Zee walks into the room, flops onto a chair near Ann, and says casually, "Boy! are you uncooperative." (He is in RI, Power Over and now feels one up.)

Ann, looking slightly perplexed, says, "Why do you say that?" (She responds as if Zee's statement were valid. She thinks Zee is in her reality of mutuality, and has *some* reason to say, "You are an uncooperative person.")

Zee is now ready to begin the battle for dominance and Power Over. To him, Ann seems open to hearing why she's an uncooperative person.

He answers her question with a touch of anger and a barely discernible note of triumph, "Because you didn't help me pick the fruit."

Ann then feels she must defend herself. She says, "But I didn't know you were picking it."

Zee snaps back, "Well, I was!"

In his mind he has won. He has just acted out the Power Over model. He has attacked Ann's basic perception of herself and she has given credence to what he said by asking, "why?" Zee is unaware of Ann's reality. Zee is feeling pretty good.

At this point Ann feels hurt and frustrated. She cannot seem to get Zee to understand that she *is* cooperative. She feels some disempowerment and some confusion about what he expected and why he didn't tell her that he wanted some help picking the fruit. She doesn't realize that this whole interaction wasn't about picking the fruit. She doesn't perceive Zee's reality at all, because he often tells her how much he loves her, and to her, love means mutual empowerment, not Power Over.

If Ann had said, "I felt hurt when you said I was uncooperative," Zee, as a confirmed verbal abuser, would have discounted her feeling by saying, for example, "You're making a big thing out of nothing!" or (sarcastically) "Well, if that's the way you want to take it, then soorrry."

Ann would be left feeling hurt and confused.

If Zee were in Reality II (Ann's reality), he would have said, "Oh, I'm really sorry, I guess I just wished you'd have known I was picking the fruit so I wouldn't have to ask you for help." Then we could say Zee really was being crabby, all right, but he regrets his irritability.

If Ann had grown up in a Reality II environment, she would have recognized that there could never be "some reason" for Zee to say "You're not cooperative." She would, therefore, have recognized that Zee was not in her reality. She would have said something like "Cut it out!" immediately. Knowing herself to be cooperative, she wouldn't accept any disparagement and she wouldn't be left with the frustration of wondering why she can't get him to understand. She would *know* he doesn't care to understand. He is more interested in, "I win! You lose!" because, after all, in Reality I that is how one feels power.

This kind of power is *not* Personal Power. It is Power Over and *Power Over is stolen power*. In Reality I, *if you don't have someone to have Power Over, you don't have any power at all.*

Another way to look at Zee's need to have Power Over is in the light of what is commonly called the "fear of being smothered." This fear is, in fact, the fear of being overpowered. In Reality I, Zee is either overpowering or believing he is being overpowered, because in this reality there is no mutuality.

Some women might live with and accept Zee's verbal jabs, and even his obliviousness to their effects. None, however, can truly live with his hostility, for Power Over is hostile. He won't change unless *he* wants to. If his partner confronts his verbal battering, if she recognizes it for what it is, if she asks for change and he refuses, if his attitude is, as one abuser put it, "I can say anything I want!" the partner may realize that he *can* say anything he wants, however, *she may also realize that there is nothing heroic about staying around to hear it.*

CHAPTER III

Personal Power: A Look at Reality II

Love is the child of freedom, never that of
domination.
— *Erich Fromm*

This chapter explores Reality II—how life is perceived and how
loving relationships exist in it. For contrast, in the next chapter we
will look at Reality I, where the abuser's struggle for Power Over,
dominance, and control prevents relationships.

Personal Power works by mutuality and co-creation. Personal Power comes from one's connection to his or her own feelings and increases through cooperation with, and participation in, life. Cooperation and participation with another person who is also grounded in his or her own feelings generate or bring into being a shared reality. This creation is the relationship itself. This is a Reality II relationship because both parties know their Personal Power. They are *mutually* supportive and empathetic. Both are living in Reality II.

A Reality II relationship is certainly desirable. If you are experiencing difficulties in your own relationship, you may be wondering, "How can I make my relationship into a mutually supportive, Reality II relationship?" It is important to know that one can't *make* this kind of relationship with another. The Reality II relationship is a shared reality. One person alone cannot create it. It takes two. Conversely, because it is a shared reality, one person alone *can* prevent it. It takes only one.

Cooperation with and participation in life include the involvement of one's self in the creative power of life. This involvement generates or brings into being a *personal reality* which can be described as the relationship one has with one's self. Through our relationship to our creative self, we experience our Personal Power. We cannot access our Personal Power when we are unaware of our feelings.

Personal Power is the ability to know, to choose and to create from the ground of one's being—from where one's feelings originate. Our feelings help us to know what we want and don't want and what gives us our greatest satisfaction.

When we have this relationship with ourselves and with the world around us, we not only experience our own creativity and Personal Power, but we also perceive the world to be a mutually supportive and creative place. Thus we describe reality in a different way than do those who would describe it as a structure of hierarchical Power Over, each level dominating the one below with human beings at the top.

Through our experience of Personal Power a new world view of mutuality and cooperation is generated. Those living in this paradigm are living in Reality II. We will look at life through this lens.

Life emerges in mystery, splendor, and infinite diversity. The old dies away, and the new is born. We grow and learn in the same way. We grieve our losses and are renewed in the process. The process of life sustains life, generates life, balances life, nurtures life, and protects life in an infinitely delicate, infinitely complex living system. *Life naturally supports life.*

One may approach the process of living and that of being in a relationship in the same way, in the way the earth builds a habitat for its creatures and its creatures in return build the earth, as for example an ecosystem thrives where all are interdependent, co-empowering each other and deriving their power from connecting with the mutually sustaining power of life in its creative and nurturing aspects.

Living in this reality requires great self-esteem and great trust in the process of life itself. It especially requires awareness of the manner and means by which those who do not share this reality may act destructively toward us. As we grow in this reality, we come to the realization that we can neither accept nor tolerate the devaluation of another person. For by such acceptance we devalue ourselves.

In a Reality II relationship, mutuality and co-creation sustain Personal Power. Both parties bring themselves to the relationship as whole and separate people. They are secure in their relationship to themselves. Because of this security, neither has a need to exert Power Over the other. Following is a description of a Reality II relationship. In this relationship each person realizes that:

To bring one's thoughts and to hear the other's,

To express one's enthusiasm and to delight in the other's,

To reveal one's self and to reflect the other,

To value one's self and to esteem the other,

To enjoy one's creations and to treasure the other's,

To pursue one's growth and to nurture the other's,

To cherish one's solitude and to honor the other's,

To follow one's interests and to encourage the other,

To act at one's pace and to accept the other's,

To indulge one's self and to give to the other,

To involve one's self and to assist the other,

To protect one's self and to comfort the other,

To see one's self and to behold the other,

To be one's self and to let the other be,

Is to love one's self and to love the other.

This is the ideal. However, in personal relationships the range of action and interaction between mutually supportive, creative relationships and destructive relationships includes a vast spectrum of possible interactions, and each interaction is of great complexity. Nevertheless, within that range we may take a broad view and mark the turning point or precise instance which indicates that the threshold has been crossed between common miscommunication and definite verbal abuse. This criterion is the intention of the communicator to inform or nurture the other versus the intention not to inform or nurture the other. *If the words or attitude disempower, disrespect, or devalue the other, then they are abusive.* Here I use inform in the broadest sense. For example, when I ask for something I am informing the other person of a desire or need. When I entertain another, greet him or her, or acknowledge him or her, in the broadest sense, I nurture him or her.

In order to recognize when one is devalued, one must have extraordinary self-esteem. A person with Reality II self-esteem knows that in her relationship she has the right to:

Respect	Shared sentiments
Acknowledgment	Kind words
Dignity	Accurate information
Esteem	Open communication
Appreciation	Attentiveness
Warmth	Caring
Empathy	Equality

In order to illustrate the self-esteem required in Reality II, let's compare responses between partners who do and do not have Reality II self-esteem.

If the partner does not have Reality II self-esteem, she thinks, "When Zee yells at me, it's because he doesn't realize that I really wasn't intending, saying, doing . . . what he says is angering him. So as soon as I explain this to him, he'll be relieved and I'll feel better, too."

If the partner does have Reality II self-esteem, the partner thinks, "When Zee yells at me, he's dumping his toxic anger on me. I'll tell him to stop it *immediately*, because there is *no* justification for his behavior." This partner has enough self-esteem to know that she will not accept being yelled at.

In a Reality II relationship, both people may make mistakes. In fact, they can expect to. However, both rest secure in their Personal Power and they can therefore acknowledge their mistakes and resolve their upsets in a *mutually* supportive way.

The partners of abusers may find it easier to evaluate their own relationships by using this model as a touchstone—something to which they can compare their own relationships, and as a reminder of what is possible in a relationship. I will continue with the premise that the abuser and his partner are living in separate realities in the next chapter, where I will describe the abuser's reality, Reality I, and the abusive relationship.

CHAPTER IV

The Abuser and the Abusive Relationship: A Look at Reality I

By uncovering the unconscious rules of the power game and the methods by which it attains legitimacy, we are certainly in a position to bring about basic changes.

— *Alice Miller*

Since recognizing and identifying verbal abuse has proven to be extremely difficult for many people, in this chapter we will explore the abuser's reality as well as the attitude or approach he takes toward his partner. This exploration will reveal some identifying characteristics common to most abusers and some conditions common to most abusive relationships.

The verbal abuser grew up in Reality I, just as the partner did. However, he never emerged into Reality II. In order to emerge into Reality II, he would have had to recognize and integrate the experiences of childhood which had left him so insecure—so in need of controlling.

The abuser lives in Reality I and values himself according to Reality I. Living in Reality I is living in the Power Over model. The abuser knows no Personal Power, nor does he experience the security and self-acceptance of Personal Power. Consequently, he avoids his feelings of powerlessness by dominating and controlling his partner. The abuser is determined not to admit to his manipulation and control. If he did, he would come face to face with his own feelings.

The abuser rejects his partner's warmth and openness, because these are the very qualities which he fears in himself. In Reality I these qualities mean vulnerability, and in Reality I vulnerability is tantamount to death.

Generally, the abuser isn't thinking about the pain he is inflicting by the abuse. He may "win" a battle with a manipulation or a convincing put-down without his partner even realizing a battle has taken place. If she does feel put down and tells him, he will deny the abuse. He might say, for example, that his partner doesn't know what she's talking about. Does she? She wonders.

In contrast, the physical abuser usually confuses his partner by admitting to his battering, apologizing, and saying he'll never do it again—then doing it again. In this case the partner ought to know that what has happened is real. She sees the scars. However, this is not always the case. As Susan Haraki, M.F.C.C., a former counselor with Battered Women's Alternatives in Concord, California, has pointed out, in some cases the abuser's denial is so deep that he can minimize the physical damage to almost nothing. This intense denial may confuse and distort the victim's own perceptions.

A partner of a verbal abuser who was in the process of recognizing that she was being verbally abused declared emphatically, "If you've never been in a verbally abusive relationship, you would have an extremely difficult time knowing what it's like. If you're in a verbally abusive relationship, you may have never recognized it."

The abuser's declarations of love are in direct contrast to the hurtful things he says. Since everyone wants to be loved, the partner is inclined to believe the abuser when he says, "I love you." After all, why would he say it if he didn't mean it? Possibly, in Reality I love means something quite different from what it means in Reality II.

All the partners I interviewed had heard two or more of the following declarations of love. Some very abusive men had frequently said them all.

Verbal abusers have been known to say:

I love you.

No one could love you as much as I do.

I'd never leave you.

I'd never do anything to hurt you.

I just want you to be happy.

It is important to remember that every person is different and every abuser is different. Some abusers may be extremely over-powering and demanding, and some may be at the opposite extreme—reclusive, only occasionally demanding, but very manipulative. Others may seem to be angry all the time. Some may involve themselves with other men, hunting or participating in other sports. Others may be loners.

The verbal abuser may show a few, many, or all of the following characteristics. Some of these characteristics, by their nature, are very difficult to recognize. Also, the abuser may describe himself as the opposite of the way his partner experiences him. For example, he may blast her with angry accusations and describe himself as easygoing. The verbal abuser may be:

1. irritable

2. likely to blame his mate for his outbursts or actions

3. unpredictable (you never know what will anger him)

4. angry

5. intense

6. unaccepting of his mate's feelings and views

7. unexpressive of warmth and empathy

8. controlling

9. silent and uncommunicative in private or, frequently, demanding or argumentative

10. a "nice guy" to others

11. competitive toward his partner

12. sullen

13. jealous

14. quick with come-backs or put-downs

15. critical

16. manipulative

17. explosive

18. hostile

19. unexpressive of his feelings

Usually the partner of a verbal abuser finds it difficult to see her mate objectively and clearly. This is especially true if she does not realize that he is, so to speak, in a different reality. He is not seeking mutuality. He is seeking to control and dominate. His behavior may be so changeable that his partner is kept off balance and is confused without knowing it. It is helpful, therefore, to consider the relationship itself.

In a verbally abusive relationship, only the illusion of an authentic relationship exists. In an abusive or Reality I relationship certain positive conditions which are intrinsic to an authentic relationship are lacking. Conversely, certain negative conditions are present. Both of these are listed below. Following this list are detailed descriptions of these conditions with examples which have been taken from real-life relationships. In a Reality I relationship

What is present is:	*What is lacking is:*
Inequality	Equality
Competition	Partnership
Manipulation	Mutuality
Hostility	Goodwill
Control	Intimacy
Negation	Validation

INEQUALITY VERSUS EQUALITY

Since the verbal abuser needs to have Power Over his partner, he cannot accept her as an equal. He may, however, tell her that he does. Why can't he accept her as an equal? Because he would experience her equality as his inferiority. He would have to ask for what he wanted. He would be open to rejection. He would have to give up control and dominance. Control and dominance seem to give the abuser a sense of power, security, and identity as a male.

One way to identify a relationship of inequality is to determine whether or not the couple can set mutual goals and discuss them together. In an abusive relationship, the couple does not really plan together. Planning together requires mutuality and equality. Mutuality and equality do not exist in Reality I. In an abusive relationship the partner may discover that her mate will not discuss long- or short-term goals with her, nor is he willing, in some instances, even to make plans with her for a weekend. Neither personal goals nor plans for the future together are discussed and agreed upon in a mutually supportive way. The following interactions illustrate the verbal abuser's unwillingness to plan with his partner.

Bella thought it might be fun to go to a nearby lake on a certain Saturday afternoon. That morning she asked, "Bert, I was wondering, do you have any plans for today?"

Bert turned angrily toward her, "Do I have to have plans?" he spit out.

"Why, no," she replied. "I was just thinking we might do something this afternoon."

"I don't see why I should have to have plans," he said, even more angrily.

"What are you mad about? I never said you had to have plans," Bella responded.

"I'm not mad! Just drop it!" Bert raged. "You said plans and *now you're trying to get out of it!*"

Bella was left feeling confused, frustrated, and upset. She wondered how she could bear feeling so badly and at the same time not be able to discuss her feelings. She knew from past experience that Bert would keep saying she was "trying to get out of it."

Bella said she had felt upset inside and had spent some time wondering what she had done to upset Bert. Had she given him the impression that she had expected him to have plans? Or, had she somehow made him feel pressured to have plans, even when she hoped he wouldn't have any and would be free?

Whenever a conversation such as this would occur, there was never anyone else around to help Bella sort it out.

Bert, on another occasion, came in from the backyard and said, "I have to replace the decks. It'll cost X dollars."

Bella, who usually paid the bills from their joint account responded, with delight, "Oh! That would be nice. We don't have that much in checking right now but we could probably get half the wood now and half later."

"If we don't have it, we don't have it!" Bert yelled angrily.

"But I'm sure we can afford it. Do you want to plan a budget with me?"

"We're not planning a budget," Bert replied angrily.

"What about the decks?" Bella asked.

"I'm not going to discuss it," Bert continued. "You spend money on anything you want."

"No I don't. Besides, I'd be happy to plan a budget with you."

With rage Bert shouted, "You're going on and on! You always have to have the last word!"

Bella confided that at this point she felt awful. She told me that she wondered how it was that she had led Bert to believe that she was trying to have the last word. She wondered why Bert would suggest that she spent too much when she knew she didn't and always checked with him regarding unusual expenses? Why wasn't he pleased that she was willing to work out a budget with him if he was concerned about expenses? Was he still planning to replace the decks? Why wasn't she able to communicate in such a way that he wouldn't perceive her as going on and on? How could she explain to him that she wanted to support him in his plans and that she was trying to cooperate?

She said that if she tried to bring up the discussion in any way, she knew Bert would tell her again that she was trying to have the last word. He said that a lot. Bella felt real mental anguish. Bert never made accusations like these if anyone else was around.

The partners of verbal abusers often spend a great deal of time trying to understand interactions similar to Bella's and Bert's. *If the partner does not know that the issue is inequality, she is left feeling confused.*

Cora told another common story of how she and Curt didn't seem to be able to plan together. In this case Curt was earning a large portion of his income from commissions, overrides, and bonuses. These earnings were community property. However, Cora never knew what her income was because she only saw a small part of it.

Cora had never been able to make plans for the future with Curt. When she signed their joint tax return and asked Curt how forty thousand dollars had been used for a business expense, he blocked all her attempts at communication with threats and accusations. (See Chapter VIII for examples of blocking.) Curt never made these accusations if anyone else was around.

Bella's and Cora's stories illustrate the frustration of inequality in an abusive relationship. Verbal abusers block discussions because they are not willing to talk with their mates on an equal basis. The abuser prevents the possibility of mutual support and planning together and so deprives himself and his partner of the many benefits such partnership would bring.

Much of the confusion that the partners experienced trying to understand these interactions would have been cleared up if they had known that the real issue was that their mates were not willing to accept them as equals.

COMPETITION VERSUS PARTNERSHIP

Competition is intrinsic to Reality I. Conversely, contributions are unacceptable in Reality I. Anything achieved by the partner is seen as a threat by the abuser. The abuser's worth is derived from a sense of one-upmanship and winning over. If the partner accomplishes something, the abuser views her accomplishment competitively. Dora tells this story:

> *While Dean was on a business trip and I was home with the children, I repainted the bathroom, which really needed it. When Dean got home I was happy to have finished it in time, as a little surprise. I wanted to tell him right away but waited until after dinner. Then, when I showed it to him saying "Look! I painted the bathroom. Doesn't it look nice!" Dean became very angry. He yelled at me, "You think you do all the work! Well, I work, too!" I said I didn't think so at all. He seemed to stay upset and angry. I couldn't get him to understand my intentions. I felt disappointment and a lot of pain, and frustration too. How did I give him the impression that I thought I did all the work? How?*

Dean never became this angry if anyone else was around.

When the partner does not recognize that her mate is angry because of his competitive approach to the relationship, she may believe, as Dora did, that she has said or done something to give him an erroneous and hurtful impression. A raging blast such as "You think you do all the work!" is accusatory and confusing, especially because it was actually Dora's feelings of mutuality and her desire to contribute which had motivated her in the first place. Her feelings and motivations were the opposite of what she was told they were. Over time this kind of abuse is killing to the spirit.

MANIPULATION VERSUS MUTUALITY

Since the verbal abuser derives his sense of power from Power Over, he feels powerless within. Feeling powerless, he may get what he wants through indirect and devious means. This is manipulation. One way of manipulating and closing off communication is to respond to the partner's attempt to discuss a problem with, "I never say anything right!" This is a covert way of saying "I can't change and I won't discuss the issue." At other times the verbal abuser may pretend not to understand or to have forgotten what his partner is talking about when she brings up an issue of deep concern to her.

There are many ways to manipulate another person, including being "friendly" only when one expects to get something from the other, suggesting disastrous outcomes to another's plans, and acting as if something has been agreed to or decided that hasn't been agreed to or decided. Following is an example of manipulative verbal abuse.

Ellen had gone back to school for her M.A. degree. She discovered that when she needed to study for finals, Ernie seemed to have very important things he needed her to do. Also, she noticed that very frequently, when she was sitting and studying, Ernie would approach her and say in a very solicitous way, expressing great concern, "Are you OK, honey?" Ellen would reply, "Oh, I'm fine. Why?"

"I just wondered if you were okay," Ernie would answer.

This occurred many times over many months before Ellen realized how uneasy she was beginning to feel about studying and how Ernie's implication that something was wrong with her when she studied was undermining her determination.

Ernie never made this comment if anyone else was around.

HOSTILITY VERSUS GOODWILL

All verbal abuse is hostile. The partners of verbal abusers are universally dismayed to realize this. "Why would he be hostile toward me?" they ask in anguish. This will become clearer later. For now, if you are with a verbal abuser, it is important that you realize you haven't done anything to make him hostile.

The abuser's hostility may be expressed overtly or covertly. He may vent his anger frequently, or he may never reveal it, preferring, instead, to manipulate and subtly control his partner.

One woman I interviewed who had left a manipulator observed that after he had broken several court orders so that he could make her life as miserable as possible, he called her and said that if she came back to him all her misery would end. He was, in fact, continuing to deny that *he* was the source of her misery.

One of the last things that a partner of a verbal abuser may realize is that her mate is hostile toward her. For example, a seemingly solicitous expression of concern such as "Are you OK, honey?" may, as shown earlier, actually be an attempt to stop the partner from engaging in a personal pursuit—certainly a very hostile action.

Hostility is expressed directly when the abuser blasts his partner. However, every blast may be so filled with accusation that the partner may believe that her mate's anger is her fault. If she accepts accusatory blame as Dora did, in all probability she would be shocked to realize that her mate is actually hostile towards her. She may have assumed all along that there is goodwill in the relationship and that he just doesn't understand her.

When there is goodwill in the relationship, there is a reaching out—a conscious concern for the other's well-being. Just as the partner asks, "What are you angry about?" her mate asks, "What is upsetting you?"

CONTROL VERSUS INTIMACY

When the verbal abuser refuses to discuss a problem, he prevents all possibility of resolution. In this way he exercises control over the interpersonal reality. Partners are frequently left with a sick, hurt feeling that is never really resolved. *There is no feeling of closure.* Upsetting incidents may reoccur in confusing flashbacks because they haven't been fully understood or resolved.

All verbal abuse is dominating and controlling. Verbal abuse used to control the partner without the partner's knowledge is called "crazymaking." "The sustaining of power seems to be one key factor in CM [crazymaking] behavior. It appears to be a way of asserting dominance while denying its existence or the wish for it." (Bach and Deutsch, 1980, p. 270)

Verbal abuse closes the door to true communication and intimacy. Intimacy in a relationship requires mutuality. Mutuality requires goodwill, openness, and a willingness to share oneself.

The abuser cannot control his partner and be intimate with her at the same time. Intimacy is lacking if there is no equality, partnership, mutuality, and goodwill. "Intimate love is fun, sexy, romantic, inspiring. Whether you have it in your relationship has little to do with how many years you have been together, but depends instead on how often and how deeply you share yourselves with each other." (Paul, 1983, p. 124)

NEGATION VERSUS VALIDATION

Because of his need for dominance and his unwillingness to accept his partner as an equal, the verbal abuser is compelled to negate the perceptions, experiences, values, accomplishments and plans of his partner. Consequently, the partner may not even know what it is like to feel supported and validated in her relationship. She may take his negation as a lack of common interest or as a misunderstanding. In truth, a verbally abusive relationship is a more or less constant invalidation of the partner's reality.

Validation is a positive affirmation of the other, such as "Yes, I understand how you're feeling." "Is this what you mean?" "I hear you."

The anguish and confusion which the partner experiences from the abuse is compounded by the abuser's negation and invalidation of both the abuse and its effects. The next chapter explores these effects. They are the consequences of verbal abuse.

CHAPTER V

The Consequences of Verbal Abuse

Oh, sir, she smiled, no doubt,
Whene'er I passed her; but who passed without
Much the same smile? This grew; I gave commands;
Then all smiles stopped together. There she stands
As if alive.
— *Robert Browning*

One of our greatest needs is to understand and to be understood. In a verbally abusive relationship, the partner's need to understand and to be understood is not met. On the other hand, her belief that her mate is rational and that understanding can be reached keeps her in the relationship.

The fact that she can't come to an understanding with her mate simply because he is abusive and will defeat her through abusive power plays is almost incomprehensible to the partner. Not coming to this realization, however, leaves the partner living in an incomprehensible reality where she is blamed for the battering of her own spirit.

Partners such as Bella, Cora and Dora, whom we met in the previous chapter, gradually lose confidence and self-esteem—often without realizing it. If they are aware of changes in their self-perception—a loss in confidence, for example—they are not aware of the cause.

This chapter discusses the consequences of verbal abuse, particularly those which concern the partner's self-perception and spiritual vitality. In addition to these consequences, partners of verbal abusers also experience emotional consequences. I have left these for the next chapter, where they are described as "The Partner's Feelings."

Following is a list of the primary consequences of verbal abuse. The partner of a verbal abuser may experience

1. A distrust of her spontaneity.

2. A loss of enthusiasm.

3. A prepared, on-guard state.

4. An uncertainty about how she is coming across.

5. A concern that something is wrong with her.

6. An inclination to soul-searching and reviewing incidents with the hope of determining what went wrong.

7. A loss of self-confidence.

8. A growing self-doubt.

9. An internalized "critical voice."

10. A concern that she isn't happier and ought to be.

11. An anxiety or fear of being crazy.

12. A sense that time is passing and she's missing something.

13. A desire not to be the way she is—"too sensitive," etc.

14. A hesitancy to accept her perceptions.

15. A reluctance to come to conclusions.

16. A desire to escape or run away.

17. A belief that what she does best may be what she does worst.

18. A tendency to live in the future—"Everything will be great when/after . . . ."

19. A distrust of future relationships.

Verbal abuse is damaging to the spirit. It takes the joy and vitality out of life. It distorts reality because the abuser's response does not correlate with the partner's communication. The partner usually believes the abuser is being honest and straightforward with her and has some reason for what he says—if only she could figure out what it is. *When the abuser's response does not correlate with her communications to him, the partner usually tries again to express herself more adequately so he will understand her.*

Since the partner does not understand her mate's motives, she "lives on hope." She clings to those times when everything seems normal and believes that, in time, there won't be so many upsets. And she may become even more hopeful if her mate says he loves her or makes some similar gesture.

Many partners said that their mates occasionally bought them gifts, shared some personal concern, or complimented them on something such as their appearance or a well-prepared meal. On these occasions their expectations rose; they forgot the past and held more hope for the future. Their hope often kept them in the abusive relationship. And the abusive relationship increased their confusion.

Following are three interactions which illustrate the kind of discrepancy between communication and response that confuse the partner. I have recreated these incidents just as they were told to me, changing only names and identifying circumstances. The partner's thoughts illustrate the effects or consequences of verbal abuse.

INTERACTION #1

Cora had been married to Curt for twenty-two years and had two nearly grown children. At the time of this interaction, she had no idea that her husband, Curt, was verbally abusive. This incident was typical of many she had experienced.

I felt a little thrill as I sensed a change in the weather. Curt had just joined me outside. I had noticed clouds moving in, and the cool moisture in the air, and I thought, "Maybe we could get a little thunder shower." I thought of the cold front moving in and turned to Curt saying, "I think maybe when weather changes rapidly from hot to cold, there's a greater chance." I was angrily interrupted with, "It's not COLD. It's COOL." "Oh," I said, "I didn't mean it's cold here." "You said cold!" Curt glared. I tried to explain, "I know it's not cold. I was thinking of weather in general and changes in the atmosphere." "Well, you didn't say atmosphere!" he raged, spitting the words out. I tried again: "What I was trying to . . ." I was interrupted again: "Will you just drop it. It's impossible to talk to you!"

I had a sick feeling in the pit of my stomach. [This is a definite sign of abuse.] I wondered, "How come I can't get Curt to understand what I'm saying? Why is it so hard? Maybe, if I'd just said I thought there was a chance of thundershowers, he would have understood."

This type of interaction never occurred when anyone else was around.

If Cora had known that this interaction was about Power Over, she would have said, "Stop interrupting me!" However, Cora believed that Curt misunderstood her and was trying to understand what she was saying, so she attempted to explain what she meant.

Let's look at the effects of this verbal abuse, knowing that, in different ways and to different degrees, Cora has lived with verbal abuse for many years.

1. Cora found that being spontaneous and open left her vulnerable to feeling hurt. (Verbal abusers abuse in cycles. The victim just recovers and forgets an abuse when another one occurs.)

2. She lost her enthusiasm.

3. Curt's unexpected anger conditioned her to be on guard.

4. Cora became uncertain about how she was coming across.

5. When Cora heard, "It's impossible to talk to you," she wondered what she was doing wrong.

6. She reviewed the incident, searching for answers.

7. Cora's confidence was undermined and her self-doubt was increased.

INTERACTION #2

Lea has been married to Luke for twelve years. They have a six-month-old child. She is an award-winning artist. He is a successful businessman. Luke is leaving on a business trip.

Luke suggests to Lea, "I can leave the Dodge (new car) with you and take the Ford (old car) when I go to the airport. There's no use leaving the Dodge in the lot where it could get damaged." Lea agrees. She cleans out the old car and they exchange keys. She drives the new car that week.

A couple of weeks pass. Luke is nearly ready to leave on another business trip. Lea thinks about cleaning out the old Ford again and asks, "Are you taking the Ford?"

Luke turns to her with a look of great astonishment and asks incredulously, "What ever makes you think I'd be taking the Ford?"

Lea is surprised, but tries to answer. "Last time you . . . ."

She is immediately interrupted by Luke, who says in a drawn-out emphatic way, "If you want . . . to drive . . . the Dodge . . . all . . . you have . . . to do . . . is ask."

The interruption throws Lea off balance. [A definite sign of abuse.] She is still trying to explain and, at the same time, a part of her mind is sorting through the previous interaction and agreement, and another part of her is filled with a feeling of striving and effort to answer Luke's question about why she thought he'd be taking the Ford. Lea says, "Luke, I'm trying to answer your . . . ."

She is cut off again with the same sentence, "If you want . . .," as if she hadn't been heard. Lea feels as if there is a brick wall between them. [Another sign of abuse.] She starts over in her thinking and realizes she doesn't want to drive the new Dodge. Luke had given her instructions about how to take care of it, where to park it, and so forth. Not wanting the responsibility or the possibility of another upset, she says, "I'll drive my car if you think it'll be OK to leave the Dodge out in the airport lot."

Luke looks at her with complete incredulity and says, "Really, the lots are perfectly safe. They *are* patrolled, you know."

At this point, Lea had wanted to remind Luke that he'd originally said he didn't want to leave the car in the lot for a week, but she stopped herself. He hadn't seemed to remember the previous discussion, and she wondered if she had not heard what she had thought she'd heard.

Lea felt distressed, but thought she probably shouldn't be. After all, if Luke had no memory of their first conversation about the car, she should accept that. "Maybe I *am* too sensitive," she thought. Later she had a strong feeling that she just wanted to run away. Life seemed so hard.

This type of interaction never occurred when anyone else was around.

Lea suffered from many of the effects of verbal abuse:

1. Lea was concerned that she wasn't as happy as she thought she should be.

2. Lea had come to believe (internalize) what the abuser had often told her—that she was too sensitive.

3. She was hesitant about her own perceptions, doubting her memory of their first conversation.

4. Lea wanted to escape or run away.

All the partners I interviewed had struggled to understand why communication was so difficult in their relationship.

INTERACTION #3

May and Mel had three children. Two were away at college. From all appearances, they had a good marriage. Mel, however, had grown gradually more abusive over the course of their relationship. May described the following:

> *Mel called and said he wanted to talk to our daughter. I told him she was in the shower, and I asked him if he wanted her to call him back. He said "yes," then added, "She called about the stereo. Tell her I don't know what the problem is." I said, "OK, I'll tell her." But then he said, "No, I could call her back later, or she could call me." I said "OK," picking up the pencil, "what message do you want me to write down." Then he blasted me with real rage: "I never asked you to write it down!" I was reeling in shock and pain. [A definite sign of verbal abuse.] At the same time, I was trying to understand why he thought I thought he'd asked me to write down the message. Everyone in the house wrote down messages for one another. All these feelings and thoughts were going through my mind at once. I could barely speak. I said, "I'll tell her you called. Bye." I hung up.*
>
> *I kept thinking, "If only I hadn't asked him what message he wanted me to write down, I wouldn't feel so bad." Somehow I must have implied a sense of obligation to him. I said it wrong. I felt like dying. [Another definite sign of verbal abuse.] I thought that if I couldn't even relate to my husband, how could I get along out in the world? I'd been thinking of going back to work.*

This type of interaction never occurred when anyone else was around.

Although Cora, Lea, and May tried to discuss these and other painful incidents with their husbands, their husbands always refused by denying, discounting, accusing, or diverting. (See Part II of Chapter VIII.)

The verbally abusive interaction, the abuser's refusal to discuss it, his denial that the upset occurred, and his implication that the partner has said "something wrong" to cause the upset all undermine her well-being. As long as the partner believes the abuser is being honest and sincere, she remains a victim of verbal abuse. As long as there is no one to validate her reality, she may remain doubtful of herself, in fear of saying or doing the wrong thing, hesitant, afraid to be spontaneous, and concerned that there is something wrong with her. *The partner who does not recognize her mate's hostility may simply assume that he just sees things very differently from her.*

SOME TYPICAL BELIEFS

The consequences of verbal abuse listed at the beginning of this chapter are intellectual and attitudinal effects. They result in beliefs that the partner may hold about herself and her relationship. Although the partners I interviewed were not always able to articulate them, these beliefs were often so deeply held that they seemed to the partner to *be* reality rather than beliefs *about* reality. Most partners held one or more of the following beliefs until they recognized that they were in a verbally abusive relationship:

The partner believed that if she were better able to express herself and to explain what she meant, her mate wouldn't be angered by her question or thought.

The partner believed that if she didn't have some inexplicable problem in perception, she wouldn't take things in "the wrong way," as she was told she did.

The partner believed that if she weren't inadequate in some way ("taking it wrong and making a big deal out of nothing") she wouldn't feel so much pain and hurt.

The partner believed that just as she was sincere and caring, the man who said he loved her was also.

The partner believed her mate was the same at work and/or with his friends and they didn't make him mad and they had no complaints, so there must be something wrong with her.

The partner believed that she was suffering needlessly because of some lack or flaw. This lack or flaw was not particularly defined but was instead a general sense of inadequacy derived from countless accusations.

Interestingly, when a verbal abuser is berating his partner, he may actually be describing himself. One partner quoted her mate's accusations thus: "You take things too seriously. You jump to conclusions. And you see everything in the worst possible light." Actually, the partners of verbal abusers consistently seem to overlook the seriousness of their own suffering and to hesitate to reach any conclusions. They are almost universally optimistic, looking for the best—seeing everything in the best possible light.

The partner believed that as soon as her mate understood that angry blasts or sarcastic put-downs really hurt her, he would stop. She reasoned that she just hadn't found a way to explain to him how much some of the things he said bothered her.

The partner believed that the way her mate was was the way men are and that she just wasn't able to understand him the way other women understood their mates.

As long as the partner does not understand the dynamics of the relationship, she does not know what to do or what is happening to her.

Many partners try to improve communication. *The partner's attempts to enhance the relationship, improve communication, and find some happiness all lead to difficulties.*

The more the partner shares her hopes and fears with the abuser, hoping for acceptance and intimacy, the more the abuser views her openness as weakness; the more superior he feels; the colder he becomes, and the more Power Over he feels.

The more the partner shares her interests and goals, the more the abuser introduces a situation or judgment which throws her off balance, diverts her from them, and reestablishes his control.

The more the partner brings up topics and attempts to engage the abuser in conversation, the more the abuser withholds, entertained by her attention and basking in the power he feels in getting it.

The more the partner accomplishes, believing the abuser will be happy for her, the more the abuser trivializes and diminishes her efforts in order to be one-up and dominant.

The more the partner lets go of her hope for acceptance and intimacy with the abuser and relies on friends for companionship, the more angry and hostile the abuser becomes.

These paradoxes demonstrate how all attempts the partner makes to grow, to be whole, and to improve the relationship bring her pain and confusion.

In summary, this chapter has explained the effects of verbal abuse upon the partner from the standpoint of her self-perception, her beliefs, and her attempts to relate to the abuser. The following chapter explores the partner's feelings.

CHAPTER VI

The Partner's Feelings

If you bring forth what is within you, what you
bring forth will save you. If you do not bring forth
what is within you, what you do not bring forth
will destroy you.
— *The Gospel of St. Thomas Logian*

This chapter explores the feelings of the partner. If she recognizes her feelings *and* knows what they tell her, she will most surely recognize verbal abuse when it occurs.

Generally, the partners of verbal abusers are aware of their feelings. However, they are more inclined to believe what their mates tell them about themselves and their relationship than what their feelings tell them about themselves and their relationship.

We have explored the abuser's reality and now might assume that since he is, in a sense, living in a different reality (Reality I), he might be the least reliable person the partner might trust to define *her* reality (Reality II). In fact, only the partner can define her reality. Her feelings are her very best guide.

For example, if, when she is upset, the partner hears, "You're making a big deal out of nothing!" or "You're taking it all wrong!" she is hearing her mate define her experience; that is, *he* is defining *her* reality. If she believes him, she will experience ever-increasing confusion. This is the essence of crazymaking and psychological abuse.

Recognizing and honoring our feelings is the way we recognize and honor ourselves and the spirit of life within us. For example, "I feel hurt. I'm being hurt" is a form of recognition. But what does it mean to honor our feelings? To honor our feelings is to give such regard to our feelings that we are able to act consciously and creatively in accordance with them to care for and protect ourselves and the spirit of life at our center.

Our feelings are sometimes very complex. They are not always easy to recognize and articulate. They are shaped by our beliefs about ourselves and about reality and they can be repressed or suppressed. The energy that our feelings carry can be acted out destructively, or can be released consciously and constructively.

Feelings can arise in the present because of an event that is occurring in the present, or because of a remembered past event, or because of events we expect or anticipate in the future. We can experience countless kinds of feelings—fear, expectancy, bliss, frustration, excitement, peace, rapture, rage, indignation, and so forth. And, just to make the situation more complex, feelings arise with varying degrees of intensity and in various combinations.

In order to simplify our look at the partner's feelings, I have selected a little more than a dozen of the primary feelings she experiences, and I discuss these feelings from one particular view or perspective. This view describes the meaning and function of feelings. It is one way to look at feelings and their meaning.

Let us imagine that there is a state of being in which one experiences clarity, serenity, integrity, and autonomy. This state of being provides one with a sense of inner security, purpose, and meaning. This state of being is called "The State of Personal Power," and the knowledge of being in that state is called the knowledge of being centered.

When two people are each in this state of being, and are also in relationship to each other, this state is magnified in each of them. They are co-empowered. In this relationship something is added. The spirit is nourished. This is the Reality II relationship I described earlier. Conversely, if one person in the relationship is not in the state of Personal Power, he will seek the experience of power through Power Over the other. In so doing he may damage his partner's connection to her own Personal Power. In this relationship something is taken away. The spirit is diminished.

In this view, being in the State of Personal Power is both a need and a right. When we are in this state, we are centered. When we are centered we feel serenity. A magnification of this state evokes such feelings as wonder, joy, and enthusiasm. A diminishment of this state evokes such feelings as sadness, frustration, and hopelessness.

When we are in the State of Personal Power we are secure. This security comes from within—from our connection to the spirit of life which is at our center. From this perspective all the varied feelings which we are capable of experiencing tell us something about our State of Personal Power and the spirit of life at our center.

Some feelings indicate harm to the spirit, just as bruises indicate harm to the body. Some feelings indicate needs of the spirit, just as hunger and thirst indicate needs of the body. Some feelings indicate activities of the spirit, just as movements indicate activities of the body. Feelings, therefore, are indicators. These indicators bring forth awareness, enabling us to recognize the condition, the needs and the activities of the spirit of life at our center.

Following is a list of the primary feelings I have chosen to review with regard to the partner's experiences in her relationship.

Responsibility	and	Inadequacy
Determination	and	Frustration
Affection	and	Rejection
Hope	and	Disappointment
Happiness	and	Sadness
Security	and	Fear
Serenity	and	Surprise/shock
	CONFUSION	

The partner may also feel shame, especially if the abuse occurs in the presence of others.

In a verbally abusive relationship the partner's feelings usually alternate and mix together and result in confusion. Now we will look at what these feelings indicate with regard to the partner's State of Personal Power and the spirit of life at her center. In this discussion of the partner's feelings I refer to the State of Personal Power as the desirable state.

RESPONSIBILITY AND INADEQUACY

The feeling of responsibility calls forth the awareness of one's ability to achieve the desirable state. The spirit is nourished.

The feeling of inadequacy calls forth awareness of one's inability to achieve the desirable state. The spirit is diminished.

Generally the partners of verbal abusers feel responsible for themselves. They try to develop themselves, to learn, and to grow. Often they are achievers whether they are at home, at work, or at school. They may also, without realizing it, feel that they are responsible for the quality of their relationship.

THE VERBALLY ABUSIVE RELATIONSHIP

For example the partner may feel responsible for the abuser's lack of understanding or for having inadvertently angered him. She may believe that she is responsible for her communications *and* for how they are taken. If the abuser seems irritated, she will try to discover what kinds of things upset him and will try to avoid them. She feels responsible for his anger because he expresses his anger in accusatory outbursts. This feeling of responsibility for another's behavior may be very difficult to recognize. Following is a personal anecdote which illustrates this:

> *Not long after I had completed my research for this book, I attended a social function and found myself in conversation with an acquaintance, a cordial businessman in his fifties. We were discussing debating teams and I said, "I would not be inclined to join a debating team until I saw how it was conducted, because I would not want to put myself in a situation that might end up with personal attacks." I explained, "I once participated in a discussion group which was not properly facilitated and I heard a man say, 'Well all you women want is . . . .' and so forth. What might have been an interesting discussion degenerated into derogatory generalizations."*
>
> *My acquaintance replied, "Ah, yes. I've seen that happen to women." I concurred that I had, often enough, and added that in relationships a lot of the time women don't even realize that they are being abused because they feel responsible for the abuse.*
>
> *"Is that so?" he asked, interestedly.*
>
> *I sought a way to illustrate my point. At that moment he glanced toward a table laid with snacks. I seized the moment. "I can give you an example. Why are you looking at the table when I'm talking to you?" This I expressed in an angry, irritated, and accusatory tone—the kind of tone a verbal abuser uses. In my intensity to give a suitable example, I must have drawn upon some latent acting talent, for he turned to me and to my dismay said most apologetically, "Oh, uh, I'm sorry, I was, ah, just looking at the cookies."*
>
> *I apologized for not having made it clear that my example was an example, and all was well. He was, himself, surprised to have been so easily "hooked" into accepting responsibility by apologizing for being berated.*

I pondered this interaction while I walked the next morning and was struck by the realization that so many of us do accept responsibility for another person's anger, *especially* when it is unexpected and completely unjustified.

I also realized that the partners of verbal abusers often say, "I was *just* . . ." And if they have been berated quite consistently, they may preface most of their actions, even when no one is around to hear them, with "I'll *just* . . .," such as "I'll *just* vacuum this room because I have a little time before I have to pick up the kids." The partner's habit of saying "I'll *just* . . .," like the businessman's "I was *just* . . .," may be a way of saying, "I hope no one will find a problem with this and berate me for it or vent their rage on me, or devise a negligent or malevolent motive for my actions."

The partner may not only feel responsible for her mate's anger, but she may also feel responsible for his happiness. This feeling of responsibility may be very difficult to avoid if the abuser manipulates his partner with a helpless, "poor-me" attitude. If she is covertly coerced she may begin to feel that she must go along with what he wants to prove her love.

The partner's feelings of responsibility alternate with feelings of inadequacy when she can't get the abuser to understand her or when she can't understand him and what he really wants or when she can't figure out why he is so often angry with her.

When the partner recognizes that she is being verbally abused, she no longer accepts responsibility for her mate's behavior. Then, by asking for changes and choosing freely the kind of life she desires, by taking responsibility for herself, and by acting in her own best interests she relieves her feelings of inadequacy and regains her natural State of Personal Power. Her spirit is nourished.

DETERMINATION AND FRUSTRATION

The feeling of determination calls forth the awareness of an intention to reach the desirable state. The spirit is nourished.

The feeling of frustration calls forth the awareness of having been kept from reaching the desirable state. The spirit is diminished.

The partners of verbal abusers are often determined to understand and express themselves more adequately in order to achieve more understanding in their relationship. Consequently, the partner may try to explain to the abuser that she isn't, for example, thinking what the abuser says she is thinking, saying what the abuser says she is saying, or acting as the abuser says she is acting; that she doesn't mean what the abuser says she means or intend what the abuser says she intends. And each time she explains what she is really thinking, doing, or saying, what she means or intends, the abuser negates her in some way. The partner is left with a deep sense of frustration.

Usually the partners of verbal abusers do not know what is going on in their relationship. They do not recognize verbal abuse. Whether they try to be completely themselves or to be as they believe their mates would like them to be, they feel frustrated. Their feelings of frustration may be difficult to identify. They do not rage, shout, scream, or nag because they do not feel their frustration as anger. They simply renew their determination to understand and to be understood.

When the partner recognizes that her mate has no determination to understand her, she has begun to understand him. And, although she may be angry, she is no longer frustrated. Relieved of her frustration, the partner has more energy to nourish the spirit of life at her center.

AFFECTION AND REJECTION

The feeling of affection calls forth the awareness of an inclination to share the desirable state. The spirit is nourished.

The feeling of rejection calls forth the awareness of having been refused. The spirit is diminished.

One of the ways the partner may express her affection and love is through sharing her joys and pleasures with her mate. In an abusive relationship, these overtures rarely succeed. In fact, the abuser may actually be angered when his partner thinks he would be pleased. Consequently, partners of verbal abusers are often left with a feeling of having said something that has been misunderstood or of having done something that is unacceptable or not worthwhile.

The abuser's indifference, criticism, disregard, and so forth are all felt as a kind of rejection by the partner—as if she, on each one of these occasions, just doesn't meet his standards. This rejection implies to the partner that she is somehow unacceptable or unworthy.

Intermittent rejection breeds confusion and uncertainty. When the partner recognizes her mate's rejection, she realizes that her joy and vitality cannot be shared with someone who would diminish it.

HOPE AND DISAPPOINTMENT

The feeling of hope calls forth the awareness that being in the desirable state is possible. The spirit is nourished.

The feeling of disappointment calls forth the awareness that the desirable state has not been realized. The spirit is diminished.

The partner of the abuser hopes that in time her relationship will improve. She may realize that communication is difficult with her mate, but she may also hope that once she understands him and he understands her they will both be happier. With the hope of preventing future abuse, she may ask, for example, that before he gets upset he ask her what she meant.

She may also hope that once he understands that accomplishing certain goals or having time to herself is important to her, he will be supportive; or she may hope that once her mate knows that some of his comments or behavior hurt or frighten her, he will apologize and stop them. After all, he says he loves her. It always seems to the partner that it is such a simple thing: that once he gets it (understands), they will have a happier, more fulfilling relationship.

Since the partner holds hope for connection, understanding, and intimacy, she is often disappointed. She may experience gestures of caring, such as gifts, or may enjoy expensive dinners which affluent abusers may provide. She may be told how much she is loved. However, the abuser's inability to accept her, his indifference, or his erratic temper swing her back from hope to disappointment.

HAPPINESS AND SADNESS

The feeling of happiness calls forth the awareness that the desirable state is accessible. The spirit is nourished.

The feeling of sadness calls forth the awareness that the desirable state is lost. The spirit is diminished.

The partner feels happy when she is pursuing her own goals and involved in her own pursuits. She also feels happy when her mate seems to understand her, talk to her, or listen to her. Her happiness turns to sadness when she realizes he has not understood her at all, or seems to be talking down to her or putting her down, or is refusing to talk to her, yelling at her, or accusing her.

The partner's sadness is often a deep emotional pain. Partners of verbal abusers describe this sadness as "a sick feeling in the pit of my stomach," "an ache in my throat," "a stab in my heart."

These feelings of sadness indicate deep harm to the spirit within. By realizing that this is so, the partner may recognize that her own feelings are telling her something quite real and quite different from what the abuser tells her. She may then realize that statements such as, "You're making a big deal out of nothing!" are not only lies, but also, in themselves, verbally abusive. By recognizing the validity of her own feelings the partner realizes where her own happiness lies—at her own center where her own spirit seeks nourishing, not disparaging, relationships.

SECURITY AND FEAR

The feeling of security calls forth the awareness that the desirable state is not threatened. The spirit is nourished.

The feeling of fear calls forth the awareness that the desirable state is threatened. The spirit is endangered.

In a verbally abusive relationship the partner may recognize some problems but may believe that they can be worked out. Over time, however, as the abuse intensifies or changes in kind, the partner may begin to fear the abuser and to realize that she is being abused. If she confronts the abuser, if he is unwilling to change, if he becomes angrier and more abusive or more manipulative and confusing, if she asks him to stop it and he refuses or continues to deny the abuse, she may grow to fear his anger and his unpredictability. At the same time she may fear the loss of love and the security she believed she had in the relationship.

By recognizing the abuse for what it is, the partner dispels the illusion of security in the relationship. When the partner is in psychological or physical danger from the abuser, her fear is very real. By acting to protect herself, the partner protects her own spirit and regains the security of her natural State of Personal Power.

SERENITY AND SHOCK

The feeling of serenity brings forth the awareness of being in the desirable state. The spirit is nourished.

The feeling of shock brings forth awareness that the desirable state has been lost. The spirit is diminished.

The partner of a verbal abuser usually feels startled or shocked when her mate is suddenly irritated or angry, puts her down, or is sarcastic. Since verbal abuse is, in essence, unexpected and unpredictable, the partner is often relaxed, serene, happy, or enthusiastic about something when she is suddenly thrown off balance, or shocked by her mate.

If the abuser does not express his anger overtly, the partner is stunned by his seeming incomprehension of her—who she is *and* what she has said. Just when she thinks he understands, he will suddenly express a completely different perception.

The unexpectedness of verbal abuse seems to isolate each incident in the partner's mind as unrelated to previous incidents. Each verbally abusive interaction seems to be about something different. Partners, therefore, may regain a sense of serenity between incidents. However, since each instance of abuse may seem to be a separate, one-time event, the partner may not only forget the previous instance, but also may find it very difficult to recognize any pattern of abuse at all.

CONFUSION
The feeling of confusion brings forth the awareness that there is, as yet, an unrecognized solution to an inner conflict.

The conflicting feelings that the partner experiences confuse her because she cannot resolve them with any insight. The solving or resolution of the inner conflict is achieved when the partner recognizes that she is being abused.

In order to understand the partner's dilemma, let us take another look at her reality. The partner of the verbal abuser is living in Reality II. She sees the world through mutuality and co-creation. However, she does not have the extraordinary self-esteem that living in Reality II requires. And extraordinary self-esteem is precisely what is required to recognize that her mate is in another reality—that he sees the world through the model of Power Over.

Unfortunately, living with a verbal abuser increasingly undermines the partner's self-esteem making recognition that much more difficult. It takes tremendous self-esteem to validate one's own reality when no one else seems to have done so. Sometimes, just a book that describes it, or knowing that one person "out there" understands can make all the difference. Sometimes, too, our dreams can bring us a realization or validation. In the next chapter we will look at obstacles to the recognition of verbal abuse as well as indicators of verbal abuse. These indicators include patterns of abuse, dreams and other signs.

CHAPTER VII

Obstacles and Indicators

To see or to perish is the very condition laid upon
everything that makes up the universe . . . .
— *Teilhard de Chardin*

Many factors contribute to the difficulty of recognizing verbal
abuse and the abuser's reality. These obstacles, which stand in the
path of recognition, appear in most abusive relationships. Once
they themselves are recognized they lose their power to prevent
awareness of abuse and become instead stepping-stones to that
awareness—each one suggesting an action or necessary change in
thinking. Here are some frequently encountered obstacles:

1. The partner has learned to overlook unkindness, disrespect, disregard, and indifference as not important enough
   to stand up to.

2. Upsetting incidents are denied by the abuser, and the partner thinks she's wrong.

3. Verbal abuse, control, and manipulation have not been
   articulated or defined for the partner, so she remains
   confused.

4. The partner thinks her feelings are wrong.

5. The partner intermittently forgets her upset feelings when
   the abuser is intermittently friendly.

6. The abuse can be very subtle—the control increasing
   gradually over time so that the partner gradually adapts
   to it.

7. The abuser controls the interpersonal communication and, therefore, the interpersonal reality by refusing to discuss upsetting interactions.

8. The abuser blames the partner for upsetting interactions, and the partner believes him and therefore thinks that they are her fault.

9. The partner has no basis of comparison—no experience of nonabusive relationships with men.

10. The abuser and partner may function very well together in their respective roles, making a home, raising a family, and "getting ahead," so the abusive nature of the relationship is overlooked.

11. The partner may be so absorbed in raising a family or developing a career that she ignores problems in the relationship, thinking that nothing is perfect anyway.

12. The partner may have never seen a model of a healthy relationship and good communication.

13. At times the abuser is not abusive. Consequently, the partner forgets the "bad times."

14. The partner is too stunned or thrown off balance to think clearly about what is happening to her.

15. The partner does not have the level of self-esteem which demands that she always be treated with courtesy and dignity.

16. The partner's reality has never been validated. Others don't see the abuse, so it doesn't seem real to her.

17. The partner believes her mate is rational in his behavior toward her, so that he has "some reason" for what he says.

18. The abuser's behavior is alternately abusive and non-abusive, so that the partner is never sure whether or not the relationship is working.

19. The partner believes her perceptions are wrong.

20. The partner may have no knowledge of verbal abuse and no appropriate models of better relationships to which she can compare her own relationship.

21. The partner may believe that the way her mate is, is the way men are, with possibly a few exceptions.

22. The partner may believe that if her mate provides for her he really loves her.

23. The partner thinks there is something wrong with her.

24. The partner believes that when her mate is angry she has somehow hurt him.

25. The partner may never have considered the question, "Am I being verbally abused?"

In summary, the partner does not realize that *an abusive personality—one that seeks Power Over another—is not capable of the empathetic comprehension that love and relationship require.*

Often, the partner of a verbal abuser does not recognize verbal abuse for what it is until the abuse changes, in kind or in intensity. If the partner does recognize the abuse and does confront her mate, the abuser who is unwilling to change usually intensifies his aggression in an attempt to regain control. He may intimidate her with angry rages or he may manipulatively play upon her feelings by, for example, telling her that she is "ruining the relationship."

If you are aware that the possibility exists that you may be in a verbally abusive relationship, you may begin to recognize the abuse by becoming aware of abusive patterns.

In order to discover these patterns, it is helpful to become very aware of your own experiences and feelings. You may need to keep a journal in order to keep your thoughts clear, to analyze your own experiences, and to record your feelings.

Some questions you might ask yourself are these:

"How often do you feel upset about what is said or not said to you?"

"What is going on in your life at the time?"

"Are there others present?"

"Are you usually alone with your mate?"

"What do you actually feel when there is an upsetting incident with your mate?"

"Do you feel confused, surprised, hurt, frustrated, diminished, threatened?"

"How do you respond?"

Following are ten patterns of abuse. Some or all of these patterns may be present in a verbally abusive relationship.

PATTERNS WHICH INDICATE VERBAL ABUSE

Pattern #1

The first pattern which the partner may recognize in verbal abuse is that the interactions which upset, hurt, or confuse her rarely if ever occur in public.

Verbal abuse, like physical abuse, often occurs behind closed doors. Even if there is a house full of people, the verbal abuse may occur when others have left the room and the partner is alone with the abuser. Secrecy is a key to the abuser's Power Over. Secrecy also intensifies the partner's confusion. The abuse may occur when a child is present. If it occurs in public, it is disguised so that others think it is in some way justified, or its meaning is known only to the partner. Going "public" is usually a sign of escalation and/or impending physical abuse.

> *Nan, married to Ned, a successful executive, shared this insight. "I was wondering why I felt unhappy around Ned, because friends said that I was married to such a nice guy, and how lucky I was. Then, as I thought about it, I realized that Ned never acted the same when they were around. I was really stunned when I realized that he must know what he's doing or he wouldn't keep it secret."*

Many of the women I interviewed were told by friends or relatives that their mates were really nice guys. In one case, the abuse was so severe and so threatening it was described to the partner as a prisoner-of-war experience by two therapists. Following her divorce, this woman's family still could not accept the reality of her experience. To them the abuser was "a really nice guy." The abuser had never acted the same way around them as he had when he was alone with his partner.

Pattern #2

The second pattern which the partner may recognize in verbal abuse is that the interaction which upsets, hurts, or confuses her is unexpected.

The incident occurs when the partner feels everything is fine. There are no arguments, nor are there any other indications that the relationship isn't harmonious. An example follows.

Cora described the following incident which brought the insight, "Something is really wrong."

> *I began to notice that when we were together, enjoying what I thought was a pleasant time, something would happen and I'd feel sick inside. I remember the time I parked the car in a dirt lot at a country craft fair. Curt asked, "Are you going to leave the parking receipt on the dashboard?" We were out of the car. I glanced around and said, "Oh, I guess not. No one else seems to have." Curt became furious and just screamed, "Quit giving me all that flack!" I was shocked. He was so unexpectedly violent. I was so stunned and felt so much pain, I couldn't even catch my breath to answer him. I was afraid. I thought, "Something is really wrong."*

Pattern #3

The third pattern which the partner may recognize in verbal abuse is that the interaction which upsets, hurts, or confuses her occurs when she is feeling happy, enthusiastic, or successful.

Ellen described her struggle to discover why she so often felt upset when Ernie was home. Her voice wavered as she told me the following:

> *At first I couldn't tell at all what was going on. Then one day I saw that there was a pattern to the upsetting times. I realized that whenever I was happy or "up" Ernie said something that really hurt, or he put me down and said it was a joke. When I saw that pattern—that when I was up I somehow got hurt—I felt a deep shock, I felt disintegrated. I was trying so hard to pull myself together that I couldn't understand how that could be happening. [after a few moments she continued] I think I came to fear letting him know when I was happy. Then, maybe, deep down, I came to fear being happy.*

Pattern #4

The fourth pattern that the partner may recognize in verbal abuse is that the interaction which upsets, hurts, or confuses her comes to seem familiar.

The abuse may seem like a reoccurring incident manifested in different ways. At its core, the verbal abuser's communication expresses an assumption about the partner that the partner cannot reconcile with her own conception of herself. She finds it difficult to identify. However, many partners and former partners of verbal abusers *have* identified it. "No matter what I do," they say, "he treats me as if I were his *enemy*." As Bella put it:

> *I realized that if I expressed a thought, Bert would argue against it. If I was waiting for an important message, he would forget to give it to me. If I told him I was unhappy about something, he would get mad. Underlying it all, it seemed like he thought I was his enemy.*

Pattern #5

The fifth pattern that the partner may recognize in verbal abuse is that the interaction which upsets, hurts, or confuses her often communicates disdain for her interests.

Dora put it this way:

> *If we were together, say, having dinner, and I just mentioned something I was really interested in, like a new course at the college, Dean would roll his eyes up, make a long face, give a sigh, and look at me with infinite boredom. If I said, "What's the matter?" He'd say, "nothing," then I'd say "well, you looked as if you were bored or something." Then he'd say, "Will you just get off my back!" This kind of conversation had hundreds of variations. They were very upsetting. Then I saw that he just wanted to put down my interests. I felt very bad that he would do that to me.*

Pattern #6

The sixth pattern that the partner may recognize in verbal abuse is that following the interactions which upset, hurt, or confuse her, her mate does not seem to seek reconciliation or even to be bothered by the incident.

Listen to Cora:

> *When I'd been really upset by Curt's yelling or sarcasm, I'd want to talk it out with him. But, when I'd approach him he'd say that there was nothing to talk about—there was no problem and he wasn't upset. He never approached me to reach an understanding.*

Pattern #7

The seventh pattern that the partner may recognize in verbal abuse is that, between the interactions which upset, hurt, or confuse her, the relationship seems to be functional.

Many partners said that, as couples, they and their abusers could entertain or shop or complete some household tasks without abuse. Consequently, they would forget what had happened, even as recently as the previous day. Some partners imagined that their relationship was really better than it was, especially if their mate's occupations took them away from home a great deal.

Pattern #8

The eighth pattern that the partner may recognize in verbal abuse is that in some way she is isolated.

Many partners experience a growing sense of isolation, especially from their own families or from like-minded friends.

Pattern #9

The ninth pattern that the partner may recognize in verbal abuse is that her mate defines her, the relationship, himself, and most often, the upsetting interactions.

The verbal abuser usually defines the partner, the relationship, himself, and the upsetting interactions in a way that is very different from his partner's experience. An explosive abuser may, for example, describe himself as easygoing. A cold, indifferent abuser may say that he and his partner have a very good relationship. An argumentative and opposing abuser may say that his partner is always trying to start a fight.

Pattern #10

The tenth pattern that the partner may recognize in verbal abuse is that she does not say to the abuser what she hears him say to her.

Abusive statements are listed in Chapter VIII. The reader might ask, "Do I say this?" or, "Is this what is said to me?" Many partners, who are constantly blamed and confused by verbal abuse, are surprised to realize that they have never said, nor would they think of saying, what is frequently said to them.

If you are or have been subject to verbal abuse, you may have identified one or more of the above patterns of verbal abuse in your relationship. If you are just beginning to recognize verbal abuse, the patterns of abuse in your relationship will usually become clearer over time.

Some partners have become more aware of their own feelings and the state of their relationship through the insight of their dreams. Although some dreams are very symbolic and seem confusing, others may be very direct. These dreams seem to bypass our beliefs about reality. Consequently, they may bring clarity to confusion.

DREAMS WHICH INDICATE VERBAL ABUSE

The following dreams are direct and need no explanation. Dora's dream:

> I woke from my dream feeling frightened. In the dream, every time I moved, Dean pushed me back. I was constricted, terribly. If I moved to the right, he held me back. I would move my arm and he would push it back. If I moved to the left he pushed me back. I was more and more frustrated and felt more and more fear. I had to keep conforming to my original position.

Bella's dream:

> I was sitting in the car with Bert. He was driving. He drove off the road over a cliff. I turned to him saying, "Did we have a good life?"

Cora's dream:

> I saw from behind a dark woman standing in front of me. Curt was talking to her. I knew he thought he was talking to me. I heard a voice say, "You must separate." I knew in the dream that she was a part of himself. In the dream I said, "Oh, that's his shadow."

Ellen's dream:

> I was parked in my car on a hill where, in my dream, I knew three murders had taken place. I suddenly realized the murderer was near. Then I felt myself being strangled from behind. I thought, "I'm the fourth." I reached up and broke the strangler's grip, worried that my fingernails would hurt his arms. I spun around. "Oh," I exclaimed, "It's Ernie!" I was shocked when I saw who the murderer was, and even in the dream I didn't want to hurt him. (Several women dreamed that they were being strangled by their mate.)

Ann's dream:

> *I was in a room. It was a small prison. Suddenly the door was open. I realized I could leave. I went out the door and then ran across the earth to the ocean. I jumped in and found myself in a boat where a room and bed were ready for me.*

Dora's dream:

> *There was a ledge on the side of a mountain. I was standing on it. I saw that the path had crumbled away behind me and that the ledge narrowed in front of me. I couldn't take one step forward or backward. I felt really afraid, because I knew I had to jump or I'd be standing there forever. I did. A whoosh of fear went through me. Then suddenly I was standing on the ground. I said: "Oh, I've landed on my feet."*

Lea's dream:

> *The mama bear came down a hill into my backyard. I heard it, so I went out to see it. Then I saw a tall thin tree start to fall as if it didn't have any roots. The next thing I saw was that the bear was lying on the ground. The tree had hit it and broken its skull open. I watched its lifeblood spill out.*

Some women who experience verbal abuse find that they symbolize their experience in a spontaneous visual image.

At times a verbally abused woman may find it easier to imagine a picture of what she feels than to put her feelings into words.

IMAGES WHICH INDICATE VERBAL ABUSE

One woman saw herself as a small child being knocked down every time she stood up or took a faltering step.

Two women who experienced verbal abuse visualized their relationship as a cat toying with a mouse before the kill.

One woman saw a thick, impenetrable glass wall between herself and her mate when she thought of her relationship.

PHYSICAL INDICATIONS OF VERBAL ABUSE

Eventually the stress of living with a verbal abuser shows up in a variety of physical symptoms. Following are comments from some of the women I interviewed:

> "You feel too exhausted. It's overwhelming to be my own person."

77

"My back keeps hurting, I know I keep clenching it up, like I'm warding off a blow, but I just can't relax it."

"I can't seem to understand him. I keep getting sick, and I'm tired when I wake up."

"I ache all over sometimes, as if I've been stuffed in a box."

"I just realized I get splitting headaches only after we've been together all weekend."

PART II

In Part I of this book we began with a broad perspective contrasting two kinds of power, Power Over and Personal Power, and we explored the two realities they generate, that is, Reality I, in which the other, the partner, is seen as the adversary to be dominated and controlled, and Reality II, in which the other, her mate, is thought of as a partner in the co-creation of a mutually satisfying life. We explored relationships in these contexts and, lastly, we became familiar with the subjective experiences of the partner of the abuser.

In Part II we shall more specifically explore verbal abuse, its characteristics, and its categories, as well as practical steps for change and recovery. We will explore some underlying dynamics in verbally abusive relationships, discuss important questions around therapeutic support, and take a close look at some of the problems children and parents face when they confront verbal abuse.

CHAPTER VIII

Characteristics and Categories of Verbal Abuse

Our sense of power is more vivid when we break a
man's spirit than when we win his heart.
— *Eric Hoffer*

Verbal abuse: Words that attack or injure, that cause one to believe
the false, or that speak falsely of one.
Verbal abuse constitutes psychological violence.

THE GENERAL CHARACTERISTICS OF VERBAL ABUSE

1. *Verbal abuse is hurtful.* It is especially hurtful when it is denied. When the partner's perception of the abuse is discounted and there is no validation of her reality, part of
   her hurt is her confusion.

2. *Verbal abuse attacks the nature and abilities of the partner.* The
   partner may begin to believe that there is something
   wrong with her or that her abilities are her failings. As
   Bella noted:

   > *I heard so often that I was a lousy driver, I really began to
   > think I had a problem driving. I think I was brainwashed. Do
   > you know what? I've been driving twenty-seven years with-
   > out an accident or a ticket.*

3. *Verbal abuse may be overt (angry outbursts and name-calling),
   or covert (very, very subtle, like brainwashing).* Overt verbal
   abuse is usually blaming and accusatory, and consequently confusing to the partner. Covert verbal abuse,

which is hidden aggression, is even more confusing to the partner. Its aim is to control her without her knowing it.

4. *Verbally abusive disparagement may be voiced in an extremely sincere and concerned way.* Ellen provides an example:

> *When he quietly and thoughtfully said, "The real reason we've never been able to discuss a book is that there are common phrases you don't comprehend the meaning of but that the average American understands," I thought, "That must be why we have so much trouble in our communication." I felt tremendous pain and despair; after all, then all my pain was my fault.*

5. *Verbal abuse is manipulative and controlling.* Usually the partner does not know that she is being manipulated and controlled. She may notice, however, that she may be living her life quite differently than she's planned, or certainly less happily.

6. *Verbal abuse is insidious.* Verbal abuse disregards, disrespects or devalues the partner in such a way that:

   a. Her self-esteem gradually diminishes, usually without her realizing it.

   b. She loses self-confidence without realizing it.

   c. She may consciously or unconsciously try to change her behavior so as not to upset the abuser, so she won't be hurt anymore.

   d. She may be subtly brainwashed without realizing it.

As Dora advised:

> *You'll never be able to tell if you're verbally abused by what your friends see and tell you, nor by what your husband says about himself and the relationship. Please emphasize in your book how very vague and subtle and insidious it is. You get conditioned to it and confused by it, and then you don't know what's going on.*

7. *Verbal abuse is unpredictable.* Unpredictability is one of the most significant characteristics of verbal abuse. The partner, as discussed earlier, is stunned, shocked, thrown off balance by her mate's sarcasm, angry jab, put-down, or

hurtful comment. No matter how intelligent, discerning, or thoughtful she is, she never really expects it, nor, for the most part, can she understand why the upsetting incidents occur or how to prevent them.

8. *Verbal abuse is the issue (the problem) in the relationship.* When a couple is having a real argument about a real issue, like how to discipline their children or how much time to spend apart or together, both parties may feel angry but they can say, "This is what I'm feeling angry about . . ." or "This is what I want," and eventually, if there is goodwill on both their parts, the issue *is* resolved. In a verbally abusive relationship there is no specific conflict. The issue is the abuse and this issue is *not* resolved. Another way to say this is that there is no closure.

9. *Verbal abuse expresses a double message.* There is an incongruence between the way the abuser speaks and his real feelings. For example, he may sound very sincere and honest while he is telling his partner what is wrong with her, or he may say "I'm not mad" while sounding very angry, or he may, for example, invite her out to dinner and then during dinner maintain an attitude of aloof, cold indifference. Partners say:

> "He tells me he loves me, and he tells me he can say anything he wants."

> "He says he's accepting of everyone but he criticizes me and won't accept my views or feelings."

> "He says he's relaxed and easygoing but he's angry and irritable every day."

> "He says he's supportive of me, but I feel isolated and lonely with him."

10. *Verbal abuse usually escalates, increasing in intensity, frequency, and variety.* For example, early in the relationship, the verbal abuser may abuse his partner with put-downs disguised as jokes and with withholding; gradually, other forms of verbal abuse are added. (These forms are described below as the categories of verbal abuse.)

In many, many cases, verbal abuse escalates into physical abuse which may also begin subtly as "accidental" shoves, pushes, bumps, etc., which then escalate into overt physical battering. One partner said that lately whenever she and her mate were standing near each other, looking at a map for example, she would find him standing on her foot. When she complained he would act surprised as if he hadn't realized it. But it happened again and again.

As verbal abuse escalates toward physical abuse, the abuser may begin moving into the partner's space. One partner said that whenever she was settled in a chair with her coffee and a pillow and then left the room for a moment, when she returned her mate had taken her chair. It did not, she said, matter which chair she had been in. He always refused to give it back. Later she noticed that he started stepping in front of her when she was approaching the refrigerator or the sink. Noting this transition from verbal to physical abuse is important because the clinical experience of therapists who treat battered women provides evidence that all battered women have been verbally abused.

VERBAL ABUSE AND POWER OVER

In general, if we look at verbal abuse as a means of maintaining control and Power Over, then in this context all of the categories of verbal abuse listed and explained below make some kind of sense because they are all ways of establishing Power Over. Does this mean that the abuser actually feels more powerful when he, for instance, subtly puts down his partner's interests? As incomprehensible as this is, it is so. Does this mean that the partner feels put down? Not always. She may feel a twinge of sadness that they cannot share this interest. She may even feel a twinge of sadness that her mate cannot enjoy this pleasure in, say, a particular artist or composer. Does this mean that her mate cannot enjoy this pleasure? Not always. He may simply find greater pleasure in feeling Power Over. She may never really know.

We will also see that verbal abuse prevents real relationships. This seems obvious. However, the partner of an abuser may live under the illusion that she has a real relationship. She may do so for a number of reasons, an important one being that, as a couple, she and the abuser may function adequately in their respective roles.

Verbal abusers generally experience many of their feelings as anger. For instance, if the verbal abuser feels unsure and anxious he may simply feel angry—possibly angry that he is feeling unsure and anxious. Yet part of being human is the ability to feel. The ability to feel, like the ability to think, is universal to the nature of humanity. Unfortunately, the abuser is generally unwilling to accept his feelings and unwilling to reveal them to his partner. He builds a wall between himself and his partner. He maintains a distance.

Why does he do this? Because in Reality I walls are required. Distance is also required. Both walls and distance keep the "enemy" from getting too close. The verbal abuser, consciously or unconsciously, sees his partner as an enemy or certainly as a threat who must be controlled. Consequently, the verbal abuser may wage a kind of war with his words—usually unbeknown to, and not understood by, his partner. His words are his weapons, and these weapons are the categories of verbal abuse.

THE CATEGORIES OF VERBAL ABUSE

1. Withholding

2. Countering

3. Discounting

4. Verbal abuse disguised as jokes

5. Blocking and diverting

6. Accusing and blaming

7. Judging and criticizing

8. Trivializing

9. Undermining

10. Threatening

11. Name calling

12. Forgetting

13. Ordering

14. Denial

15. Abusive anger (this is addressed in Chapter IX)

1. WITHHOLDING

If there is a relationship, then there must be more than the exchange of information. A relationship requires intimacy. Intimacy requires empathy. To hear and understand another's feelings and experience is empathetic comprehension. The intimacy of a relationship cannot be achieved if one party is unwilling to share himself and is unable to support his partner in an empathetic way. Although two people may not always understand each other or may have difficulty expressing their feelings, the intention to understand is there if both parties can say, for example, "Is this what you mean?" or "Is this how you feel?" or, "I think . . ." or "I feel . . ." One person cannot create intimacy in a relationship.

The abuser who refuses to listen to his partner, denies her experience, and refuses to share himself with her is violating the primary agreement of a relationship. He is withholding.

Withholding speaks as loudly as words and is a category of verbal abuse. Simply put, withholding is a choice to keep virtually all one's thoughts, feelings, hopes, and dreams to oneself and to remain silent and aloof toward one's partner, to reveal as little as possible, and to maintain an attitude of cool indifference. A confirmed verbal abuser may go for months or years without attempting to engage his partner and without empathetically responding to her.

Withholding can go on for years because the partner, after trying to engage her mate, may assume that he is, after all, a very quiet person, or totally self-contained or, maybe, extremely shy, or has some "hang up," or is, maybe, slightly autistic. She can conjecture any one of these reasons for the verbal abuser's behavior more readily than she can conceive of his reality.

Although the partner may wish for more companionship and conversation, she may decide that she cannot expect more than it is within her mate to give. She may never doubt for a minute that he really does want to share himself with her. "He's just shy about it," some partners say. The following interaction between May and Mel illustrates this situation very accurately:

> One time I heard Mel tell his brother that he wondered what a certain actor was thinking during a dramatic scene in a movie we'd seen recently. (I really couldn't recall Mel ever saying he wondered about anything before.) Later that evening I told him that I'd heard him mention this, and that I thought it was wonderful that he was expressing his thoughts that way, and that I'd love to have him share that kind of thing with me.
>
> I thought now, at last, he'll understand. I have a concrete example for him. And not only that, I also thought that his

sharing what he wondered about was probably a real break-through for him. He'd always been so silent, except for jokes and occasional comments, that I had come to think he was sort of autistic. I told him that he might not have realized it, but I really was interested in his thoughts. I believed that if I told him that what he had said to his brother was the kind of thing I wanted him to share with me, he would understand and would talk to me. He never really did.

What confused me was that he said, "Oh, OK, I didn't think you'd be interested," as if he understood, but he never really seemed to understand.

Cora had a similar experience. She said, "I didn't know what to do. For a while there, I thought that if I were somehow more interesting or entertaining or more intelligent or more well-read or more educated or something, he'd talk to me once in a while." Thoughtfully, she continued: "I guess I really started thinking something was wrong when I was over at a friend's and her husband came in and started telling her about a fellow he met at the tennis court. I couldn't remember Curt sharing like that. Being with Curt was a lonely experience."

The verbal abuser who chooses to withhold can add a variety of flourishes and camouflages to his withholding, such as pretending not to hear, picking up something to look at while his partner is sharing something or watching television while saying, "Go ahead, I'm listening."

The verbal abuser who chooses to withhold will respond to requests for communication with:

"There's nothing to talk about."

"What do you want me to say?"

"What are you complaining about; I do talk to you."

"You never let me talk."

"Why should I tell you if I like it; you'll do what you want anyway."

"You wouldn't be interested."

These responses, of course, add to the partner's confusion. She may believe the relationship is functional because the abuser may communicate functional information. However, the relationship is dysfunctional because there is no intimacy. Functional information is, of course, important, but it cannot be the only form of communication if there is to be a real relationship. Two other kinds of communication are also important. These are communications which engage another and communications which respond to another. Following are three lists which illustrate these three kinds of communication:

Communication of Functional Information

I'll be late tonight.

The list is on the table.

Do you need some help with that?

Who left that out?

Where's my hammer?

Please leave my mail here.

The show is on now.

The light is broken.

The car is almost out of gas.

Communication Which Engages Another

A penny for your thoughts.

Guess what happened on the way to . . .

I was thinking . . .

Did you ever wonder . . . ?

What's your favorite . . . ?

How did you like . . . ?

What I like best about . . . is . . .

I feel . . .

What would you like to be doing a year from now?

What do you think about . . . ?

When you're free, would you mind talking this over with me?

Communication Which Responds to Another

Oh, I see what you mean.

Yes, I understand.

That's interesting.

I hadn't thought of that.

Uh huh.

Oh! I've always looked at it this way.

It sounds like you're saying . . . .

I'll think it over and let you know.

What did you have in mind?

Are you saying . . . ?

Oh! Do you mean . . . ?

2. COUNTERING

Countering, another category of verbal abuse, is the dominant response of some verbal abusers. Since the abuser is in Reality I, he sees his partner as an adversary. How dare she have a different view from his? If she sees things differently, he may feel he is losing control and dominance of her. Consequently, he may choose to argue against her thoughts, her perceptions, or her experience of life itself. As a category of verbal abuse, countering is one of the most destructive to a relationship because it prevents all possibility of discussion, it consistently denies the victim's reality, and it prevents the partner from knowing what her mate thinks about anything. An abuser who constantly counters seems only to think the opposite of his partner. She cannot know what he really thinks about anything. Therefore she cannot know him. A withholder-counterer is almost unknowable.

In Chapter V, interaction number 1, Curt countered Cora when Cora said, "I think maybe when the weather changes rapidly from hot to cold . . . ." At that moment Curt countered with, "It's not cold! It's cool!" In this interaction Curt countered Cora as if she had actually said it was cold. A verbal abuser may be so quick to counter his partner, he cannot hear her or allow her to finish her thought and, certainly, he cannot discern her tone of voice.

Notice also that when Cora said "I think maybe . . ." Curt could not allow Cora to have her own thoughts or her own view. When a verbal abuser counters his partner he does not preface his response with any phrase like, "It seems to me . . ." or, "I think . . ." or, "I feel . . ." He simply says that what his partner has said isn't so. A confirmed verbal abuser who chooses countering as a means of domination and Power Over counters his partner's thoughts, beliefs, and feelings. If she says, "It seems to me that . . ." or "I feel . . ." or "I think . . ." in his presence, usually she will be countered.

Cora explained her experience of Curt's opposition:

> *If I say anything directly or express my thoughts on something, Curt says it's the opposite. I feel like I can't say anything without it being put down. I don't think there's anything I can say that he won't counter. What he's really saying is "No, that's not the way it is," even about my most personal experience of something.*

Following are some additional examples of countering:

Interaction #1

Abuser: The scene change took too long.

Partner: Oh! I didn't notice that.

Abuser: You're wrong.

Partner: Well, I mean it felt fine to me and I guess it didn't to you.

Abuser,
angrily: You don't know what you're talking about! There is an objective reality, you know. Any critic would agree with me!

This partner tried to explain to her mate that she simply had a different experience from him. He told her that both her experience and her feelings were wrong. She said that he was so angry she thought they must be wrong.

Interaction #2

Partner: It seems to me that we're spending too much on arms and not enough on education.

Abuser: That's not so and you can't get any statistics to prove it.

Interaction #3

Nan recognized countering when she had the following interaction. She agreed with Ned, repeating a statement he'd made, and then she noticed that Ned immediately countered the statement. She then repeated his counter, agreeing with it, and Ned countered that. Here is the interaction:

Ned: That lamp shade doesn't go with the lamp.

Nan: Oh, yeah, the lamp shade doesn't go with the lamp.

Ned: It does too go with lamp.

Nan: Oh, the shade goes with the lamp.

Ned: You can't say it goes with it when the color's off.

Nan: Oh. I see, the color is off.

Ned: That's not what's wrong with it.

Nan: I'm trying to find out what you mean.

Ned: No, you're not. You're twisting my words around!

As strange as this interaction is, it is not at all uncommon. Countering truly blocks all communication and all possibility of intimacy.

3. DISCOUNTING

Discounting denies the reality and experience of the partner and is extremely destructive. If the partner does not recognize it for what it is, she may spend years trying to figure out what is wrong with her or what is wrong with her ability to communicate. Discounting denies and distorts the partner's actual perception of the abuse and is, therefore, one of the most insidious forms of verbal abuse.

One way to understand discounting is to imagine an item in a store worth one hundred dollars discounted to one cent. In this imaginary example, the item is discounted to the extent that it is deemed valueless, worth nearly nothing. In reality the verbal abuser discounts his partner's experience and feelings as if they were worth nothing.

If the partner says, for example, "I felt hurt when I heard you say . . ." or "I don't think that's funny, it feels like a put-down" or "I feel bad when you yell at me like that," the abuser may discount his partner's feelings, saying something that gives her the message: "Your feelings and experience are wrong, they are worth nothing." Following is a list of common discounting statements:

You're too sensitive.

You're jumping to conclusions.

You can't take a joke.

You blow everything out of proportion.

You're making a big deal out of nothing.

You don't have a sense of humor.

You see everything in the worst possible light.

You take things too seriously.

You feel too much.

Your imagination is working overtime.

You don't know what you're talking about.

You think you know it all.

You always have to have something to complain about.

You're trying to start something.

You're not happy unless you're complaining.

You take everything wrong.

You're making a mountain out of a molehill.

You read things into my words.

You twist everything around.

You're looking for a fight.

It is not unusual for the partner to trust the abuser. She may believe, for example, that something is intrinsically wrong with her or her sense of humor or her perceptions. These beliefs can lead to feelings of frustration and futility. She may spend hours trying to figure out how it is that she comes across the way he says she does, not realizing that his discounting statements are said to avoid having to take responsibility for his behavior.

4. VERBAL ABUSE DISGUISED AS JOKES

Abuse disguised as a joke is a category of verbal abuse which all of the women I interviewed experienced. It takes a quick mind to come up with ways of disparaging the partner either crassly or with wit and style. This kind of abuse is not done in jest. It cuts to the quick, touches the most sensitive areas, and leaves the abuser with a look of triumph. This abuse never seems funny because it isn't funny.

Disparaging comments disguised as jokes often refer to the feminine nature of the partner, to her intellectual abilities, or to her competency.

If the partner says "I didn't think that was funny," the abuser may, for example, discount her experience by angrily saying, "You just don't have a sense of humor!" or "You just can't take a joke!" or he may accuse her of antagonism by angrily saying, "You're just trying to start an argument." These statements themselves are abusive.

It may be obvious to the reader that the abuser's responses do not demonstrate goodwill or an interest in the relationship. Unfortunately, the partner is usually not that clear about it. Since the abuser responds with anger, the partner may believe she did "take it wrong" and *that* is what he's angry about, or (as some partners of abusers do) she may wonder if there is something wrong with her sense of humor. The brainwashing effects of verbal abuse cannot be overemphasized.

Following are disparaging comments which a verbal abuser will describe as a joke:

You need a keeper!

Boy! are you easily entertained.

What else can you expect from a woman?

You couldn't find your head if it wasn't attached.

An abuser may also startle or frighten his partner, after which he will laugh *as if* it were a joke.

5. BLOCKING AND DIVERTING

Blocking and diverting is a category of verbal abuse which specifically controls interpersonal communication. The verbal abuser refuses to communicate, establishes what can be discussed, or withholds information. He can prevent all possibility of resolving conflicts by blocking and diverting. Blocking may be by direct demand or by switching the topic.

Blocking may also be accusatory; however, its primary purpose is to prevent discussion, end communication, or withhold information. Examples of blocking are:

You're just trying to have the last word!

You know what I meant!

You think you know it all!

You heard me. I shouldn't have to repeat myself!

You're talking out of turn!

I don't see where this is going! The discussion is ended!

That's a lot of crap!

Quit giving me all that flack!

Will you get off my back!

Just drop it!

You always have to be right!

Quit yakking!

Did anybody ask you?

Where did you get a crazy/stupid/weird/dumb idea like that?

Who asked for your opinion?

Quit your bitching!

Blocking can also be accomplished through diversionary tactics. For example, in the interaction in Chapter IV, when the partner asked how the $40,000 was spent, the abuser blocked her attempts to gain information by diverting her from the issue with accusations and irrelevant comments.

Often the partner does not notice that the original topic is no longer the topic. She has been diverted.

Following are examples of blocking by diversion. All may be used to divert the partner from the legitimate question, "What happened to the $40,000?"

What are you worried about! you have plenty to spend!

There's no way I'm going to go through all those receipts!

It costs money to stay in business so quit harassing me!

I'm not going to try to explain to you how the corporate retirement programs are set up!

Don't complain to me till you're earning two hundred thousand a year!

I've explained it all to you before, and I'm not going to go through it again!

All you married me for is my money!

Do I have to account for every penny!

How about you accounting for every penny you spend!

You're always trying to start something!

I'm sick of your complaints!

If you think it's so simple, then you can do the taxes and I'll quit work!

Just drop it. I don't need that kind of hassle!

It's too complicated for you to understand!

Diverting invites a response from the partner such as, "I'm not complaining, I'm simply asking a question" or "But I don't know what receipts you're talking about." Through diversion the topic is changed. None of the abuser's diversions answer the partner's question in a thoughtful and considerate way.

6. ACCUSING AND BLAMING
A verbal abuser will accuse his partner of some wrongdoing, or of some breach of the basic agreement of the relationship, blaming his partner for his anger, irritation, or insecurity. Some examples follow.

Partner: Somehow I feel closed off from you.

Abuser,
furiously: I don't need to be attacked like that!

95

In this interaction the verbal abuser accuses his partner of attacking him. In this way he avoids all intimacy and all possibility of exploring his partner's feelings.

Abuser: Where's my wrench?

Partner: I think the kids left it in the back of the car.

Abuser
angrily: I never asked you!

Partner: What are you so angry about.

Abuser with
rage: You *knew* it was a rhetorical question!

The partner is accused of responding to an expression "phrased as a question only for dramatic effect and not to seek an answer" (*Oxford American Dictionary*). Also, the abuser is blaming his partner for his anger by telling her that she knew she wasn't supposed to answer.

Partner: Honey, I'm real tired tonight.

Abuser: If you're not getting it from me, then tell me who you're getting it from.

The partner's communication is not accepted, and she is accused of infidelity and thus blamed for the abuser's insecurity. The implication is meant to goad her into submission.

Following are some abusive, accusing and blaming statements. To most partners they are very painful because usually the partner wants more than anything to assure her mate that she is not his enemy:

You always have to have the last word.

You're just trying to pick a fight.

You're looking for trouble.

You're attacking me.

You can't leave well enough alone.

I've had it with your attacks/bitching/complaining.

7. JUDGING AND CRITICIZING

The verbal abuser may judge his partner and then express his judgment in a critical way. If she objects, he may tell her that he is just pointing something out to be helpful, but in reality he may be expressing his lack of acceptance of her. Most verbal abuse carries a judgmental tone. For example, comments which negate the partner's feelings, such as "You're too sensitive," are judgmental, as are abusive "jokes." Following are some examples of judgmental criticizing:

Statements which begin with "The trouble with you is . . ." are judgmental, critical, and abusive.

Statements which begin with "Your problem is . . ." are judgmental, critical, and abusive.

Most "you" statements are judgmental, critical, and abusive. Some abusive judging and criticizing "you" statements are:

You cheat.

You're never satisfied.

You're a lousy winner.

You're stupid.

You can't take a joke.

You're crazy.

You can't let well enough alone.

How dumb (you are).

How stupid (you are).

Critical statements made about you to others are abusive. These are "you" statements turned into "she" statements. Following are some examples:

She's afraid of her shadow.

She can't keep anything straight.

She never sticks to anything.

She never stops nagging.

She doesn't know if she's coming or going.

Critical "stories" about your mistakes or actual lies about you which embarrass you in front of others are abusive; for example,

She's a white-knuckle flier.

She sweeps the dirt under the carpet.

Every time she goes out to the mall she forgets her wallet.

Statements which criticize specific words out of context are abusive; for example,

Cora and Curt are getting ready for a ski trip.
Cora exclaims with anticipation, "I can't wait to drive up there!" Curt responds curtly, "You're not driving. I'm driving!"

Dora comes into the family room during a commercial and asks Dean, "Is the program over?" Dean replies angrily, "It's not a program! It's a playoff!"

In both of these examples the partner feels frustrated and finds herself saying, "That's not what I meant." Her meaning is already known to the abuser. He's in Reality I and in this reality making his partner *wrong* gives him a sense of Power Over her. This type of abuser is likely to frequently tell his partner she always has to be *right*.

Criticism disguised as help or advice is abusive. Some examples follow:

Wouldn't it have been better to . . .

If you'd have . . . it would have turned out better.

This would have been a better way.

I wouldn't do it that way if I were you.

Next time you should . . .

You should have used . . .

Look what you missed.

8. TRIVIALIZING

Trivializing says, in so many words, that what you have done or expressed is insignificant. When trivializing is done in a frank and sincere tone of voice, it can be difficult to detect. If the partner is very trusting, she may listen with an open mind to the abuser's comments and end up feeling perplexed that he doesn't understand her or her work or her interests.

Trivializing can be very subtle, so that the partner is left feeling depressed and frustrated but isn't quite sure why. Following is an example of trivializing in the relationship of Ellen and Ernie:

I spent several weeks going through the papers and old household files that Ernie and I had accumulated over more than twenty years. After extensive sorting, I categorized everything and made color-coded files: Business, Medical, Insurance, Personal, etc. The result was three drawers of files in a new file cabinet. It was a long and tedious job.

Occasionally I had mentioned to Ernie how the work was progressing. Finally, after a couple of weeks' work, I was glad to be done. I said, "Ernie, I finished the files. It was really a job." I opened the drawers and showed him what I'd done. He said, "Wow! I'm impressed." I didn't remember him acknowledging me like that ever before. With a smile I said, "You are?" He answered in a strange voice "I'm impressed with how you got those names to fit on all those little itty bitty labels." I said, "Oh, Ernie, I just typed them on. That wasn't the hard part." He looked seriously at me and said, "Well, I think it was."

I felt sad and I felt frustrated. I wondered why it was so hard for me to talk with him. Why couldn't I get him to understand about the work I'd put in? I knew he'd typed names on labels before. I couldn't see why he'd think it was so much harder than the weeks of sorting and organizing, especially since many of the names were abbreviated. I felt that I just couldn't get across to him what I was really feeling.

This verbal abuse set up the partner for extra hurt. Feeling a sense of her mate's pleasure in, and approval of, her work, the partner was very open and vulnerable to the trivialization of it. First the abuser said he was impressed, then he commented on the smallest thing about it, refusing to acknowledge the effort or the results.

Lea described another experience of trivializing:

The other day I achieved an effect in my painting I had been striving for. That evening I mentioned to Luke that I'd finally got my painting to work the way I wanted, and he said in a really sarcastic voice, "Well, isn't it nice to have something to do in the daytime." I felt very frustrated. I can never seem to get him to understand how important my work is to me and that it's not just something to do in the daytime.

Trivializing is confusing to the partner because, if she doesn't recognize it for what it is, she believes she somehow hasn't been able to explain to her mate just how important certain things are to her. The abuser may feel one up when he puts his partner down, but his partner is kept on an emotional roller coaster.

9. UNDERMINING

Undermining not only withholds emotional support, but also erodes confidence and determination. The abuser who undermines his partner has usually verbally abused her in many other ways. Consequently, her self-esteem and confidence are already low, making her that much more vulnerable to the abuse. Comments such as those below, which dampen interest and enthusiasm, are examples of undermining:

Partner: What a pretty flower!

*Abuser, with
    disgust:* A flower's a flower.

Partner: I'd like to find out if there are any . . .

Abuser: What's the point?

   OR Why bother?

   OR I don't see that that'll get you anywhere.

   OR Who cares?

Direct squelches such as the following are also undermining:

Who asked you?

Nobody asked your opinion.

You always have to put in your two cents!

You wouldn't understand.

It's over your head.

You'll never make it.

You couldn't talk if your hands were tied.

What makes you think you're so smart?

Whom are you trying to impress!

Sabotaging is also a way of undermining; following are some examples from interviews with Dora and May:

> I was feeling really good when I told Dean that I had thought of a plot for a story I thought I'd like to write. He listened and then said, "Really, I don't know anyone who would be interested in reading it." I sort of lost my enthusiasm.

> I had an idea for a diet and health workshop. The day after I'd told Mel about it he handed me an article he'd found and said, "This seems to cover all the bases." The article described everything I was interested in for the workshop as faddish, and it described the people who were interested in diet and health as fanatics. I felt very strange. I couldn't get my motivation up or get going on it.

In Chapter IV we read about Ellen's experience of being asked whenever she was studying if she was all right. She began to feel as if something were wrong—an anxiety about studying. It was only with outside intervention that she recognized the source of her anxiety. This kind of sabotage undermines the partner's determination and sense of well-being.

Another form of sabotage is disruption and interruption. For example, the abuser may sabotage his partner's conversations with others by causing some disturbance such as breaking into uproarious laughter or walking into the room and pounding on the piano, as did one abuser. He may also simply interrupt her by finishing her story, opposing her, or negating her.

Undermining may imply to the partner that she is inadequate. An example follows, courtesy of Bella:

> I said, "I'll need to read this before I sign it." Then Bert got angry and said, "Well it seems like a simple thing to me."

Here Bert implies, "I can think for you. It's too complex for you."

10. THREATENING

Threatening manipulates the partner by bringing up her greatest fears. Verbally abusive threats usually involve the threat of loss or pain.

Some examples follow:

Do what I want or I'll leave.

Do what I want or I'll take a mistress.

Do what I want or I'll get a divorce.

Do what I want or I'll really be angry.

Do what I want or I'll hit you.

OR

If you . . . , I'll . . .

11. NAME CALLING

Name calling is one of the most overt categories of verbal abuse. *All* name calling is verbally abusive. Forms of endearment such as "sweetheart" are, of course, excepted, unless said with real sarcasm.

12. FORGETTING

Forgetting involves both denial and covert manipulation. The declaration by the abuser that what occurred didn't occur is abusive. Everyone forgets what happened now and then. However, consistently forgetting interactions which have a great impact on another person is verbally abusive denial.

Often, after the partner collects herself after being yelled at or put down, she may try to talk to her mate about it. He will have conveniently "forgotten" the incident, saying, for example, "I don't know what you're talking about. I'm not going to listen to this."

Some abusers seem to *consistently* forget the promises which are most important to their partners. Often the partner is truly counting on a very important agreement made by her mate. He will have "forgotten" the agreement. "I don't know where you got that" or "I never agreed to anything" are common forms of denial.

13. ORDERING

Ordering denies the equality and autonomy of the partner. When the abuser gives orders instead of asking respectfully for what he wants, he is treating his partner as if she were the glove on his hand, automatically available to fulfill his wishes. Following are some examples of ordering:

Get rid of this.

Get in here and clean this up.

You're not going out now.

Get this off of here.

You're not wearing that.

We won't discuss it.

Shut that off.

We're doing this now.

14. DENIAL

Although all verbal abuse has serious consequences, denial is one of the most insidious categories of verbal abuse because it denies the reality of the partner.

A confirmed verbal abuser may use every form of verbal abuse on a regular basis. This very same abuser might very well read this section on the categories of verbal abuse and say that he has never been abusive, that he loves his partner, and that he would never do anything to hurt her. *This is denial:*

I never said that.

You're making that all up.

We never had that conversation.

You're getting upset about nothing.

I don't know where you got that.

You've got to be crazy.

These are all examples of denial.

THE VERBALLY ABUSIVE RELATIONSHIP

When the partner of the abuser clearly realizes that

He *did* say that.

She's made *nothing* up.

They *did* have that conversation.

She's upset about *something*.

Her experience *is* real.

She's *not* crazy.

Then, she has enough self-esteem and knowledge to recognize verbal abuse.

ABUSIVE ANGER

This category of abuse is the subject of Chapter IX.

CHAPTER IX

The Anger Addict

We can't do without dominating others .... The essential thing, in sum, is being able to get angry without the other person being able to answer back.
— *Albert Camus*

Anger underlies, motivates, and perpetuates verbally abusive behavior. Abusive anger is a category of verbal abuse. In order to recognize abusive anger, it is essential that the partner fully realize
that she is in no way responsible for being yelled at, snapped at,
raged at, or even glared at—no matter how demanding, accusing,
or blaming the abuser is. This means that, since she is not responsible in any way for the abuse, she need in no way defend herself
by explaining herself. She may protect herself, however, as Chapter XI will describe.

The partners of verbal abusers know that explaining what
they really said, meant, or did has never brought an apology such
as "Oh, I'm so sorry to have snapped, shouted, or yelled at you.
Will you forgive me?" The partners of verbal abusers know this
from experience. But they hope that they will not have to give up
the hope that *this time* he will understand. This hope may be the
hardest of all hopes to give up.

In Chapter II I gave an example of what happens when the
partner defends or explains herself. What happens is that she steps
back toward the abuser's reality. He then thinks she is in his reality, where battles are the norm, and he really starts to battle her.
Apologizing is the last thing on his mind.

It is also important for the partner to fully realize that there is
no "way she can be" to prevent the abuser from venting his anger
on her. Speaking more gently, listening more attentively, being

more supportive, more interesting, more learned, more fun, thinner, cuter, or classier—being more anything will not work.

The abuser's anger arises out of his general sense of Personal Powerlessness. He expresses his anger either covertly through subtle manipulation or overtly in unexpected outbursts directed at his partner. These outbursts accuse and blame the partner. By making her his scapegoat, he denies the real cause of his behavior and convinces himself and usually his partner that she has somehow said or done something to justify the abuse.

When the abuser vents his anger on his partner, he releases the underlying tension he feels from his sense of Personal Powerlessness. As a result, *the partner feels bad* and *the abuser feels good*.

Attempts by the partner to find out what is wrong simply do not work. The abuser will deny his anger outright or claim that his partner is to blame for his behavior. If the abuser were to admit that his partner were not the cause of his anger, he would have to face himself and his own feelings. In most cases, abusers are unwilling to do this.

Most verbal abusers are filled with inner tension, which they periodically and unpredictably release with angry outbursts directed at their partners. The tension then builds again until the abuser releases it again with another outburst. This build-up of tension and its release become a cyclical pattern of behavior. As soon as the tension is released, it begins to build again. I call this cycle the *cycle of anger addiction* and the abuser who follows this pattern of behavior an *anger addict*.

The cycle, however, is not regular. It is not predictable. The abuser doesn't vent his anger at his partner every morning, or every evening, or every Saturday night. The intensity of the angry outbursts also varies. Factors affecting the cycle include: opportunity, changes at work or at home, the thoughts of the abuser, his current sense of power, his fears, his feelings of dependency, and his feelings of inadequacy. If he drinks, alcohol may play a part. Alcohol doesn't make him angrier so much as it makes him feel freer to vent his anger.

This cycle carries a double reward for the abuser. The rewards are like a fix for an addict. The first reward is that the abuser feels a sense of relief, a kind of euphoric high after exploding at his partner because he has released the tension built up since the last outburst. The second reward is that he has reasserted his dominance and Power Over his partner. *There is nothing she can do and no way she can be to prevent the next attack.*

The partners of anger addicts try many ways to deal with the unexpected blasts. Since the abusers are blaming and accusing, the partners may believe that they are somehow to blame. Eventually, without realizing it, they may end up living in a prepared "on-guard" state. Coping may become a way of life without the partner realizing it. Not only is the partner affected by the abuse but also, at some level, all members of the family are affected.

May told me how true this was for her. As she talked about her family she said, "He saw me crying. He said, 'What happened?' I told him I'd just got yelled at. He said, 'Mom, as soon as you hear Dad's voice on the phone you've got to be prepared with your finger on the button ready to hang up. Don't spend any time trying to figure out what he's saying. *As soon as you hear the anger, hang up.* Then you'll be laughing instead of crying.'"

The verbal abuser's anger is free-floating and irrational. It has nothing to do with the partner. It does, however, affect her deeply. Being verbally shouted at, raged at, or snapped at leaves the partner in pain and confusion. These attacks throw her off balance. They disrupt her equilibrium and batter her spirit. Although they have nothing to do with the partner in their origin, they hurt her, because hostility against another human being, whether it is physical or emotional, is painful.

Some partners have tried to ignore their mate's angry outbursts, thinking, "I am strong. He doesn't really mean it. I won't let him get me down. Sooner or later I'll understand him better, or he'll understand that certain things he says bother me, or he'll learn to ask me what I did/said/meant before he gets mad." What happens as a result of this approach? The partner uses her strength against herself. She struggles to stay balanced and serene while using her strength to endure and to try to understand the abuse. She may suffer from traumatic shocks. And, certainly, she becomes more confused. As Ann put it, "He loves me. He just doesn't like me."

Also, if the partner calmly endures the abuser's behavior, he will feel thwarted. He expects a reaction. He needs his fix of both the release of tension *and* a sense of Power Over his partner. If he hasn't gotten his partner down, if she shows no signs of losing her enthusiasm, he will increase the abuse. This is probably not a conscious decision. He's just angrier, more tense, and more dependent on his fix of Power Over. This is one of the reasons that verbal abuse increases over time. As the partner adapts—trys to ignore the behavior, possibly hoping it will stop or hoping she won't in-

advertently provoke him or that she'll figure out what she's "doing wrong" or why she's "feeling wrong," the abuser increases the
intensity and/or the frequency of the abuse.

Another reason that verbal abuse increases over time is that
the "fix" never really fixes anything. The abuser's lack of a sense
of Personal Power and consequent need for Power Over persist.
Through time, these pressures increase, and as a result the
abuser's anger and hostility increase.

As the partner uses her strength to ignore the outbursts or to
make sense of the relationship or to hope that it will get better, the
abuser uses his strength to increase the abuse. If the partner tells
her mate how upsetting his outbursts are to her, she will usually
face an intense angry denial telling her that she's overreacting.

One of the reasons anger addicts don't apologize is that to
sincerely do so would entail giving up the fix. The fix—the explo-
sion and release of tension—allows the anger addict to maintain his
equilibrium. It also gives him a high and a sense of Power Over. For
as long as he can deny his responsibility for his anger and can accuse
his partner of causing it, the abuser can continue to maintain his equilibrium and to get a high at his partner's expense.

The partners of anger addicts and verbal abusers in general
are consistently shocked to realize that their mates feel good when
they feel so hurt. Cora's experience demonstrates this:

> *I told Curt I had felt bad all day about the argument
> we'd had that morning. (He had just blasted me for no reason.
> I had tried to reason with him, and he'd just walked out and
> gone to work.) He said, "What argument? I don't know what
> you're talking about." I reminded him of how angry he'd
> seemed that morning when he was yelling at me about how I
> fixed the eggs. I asked him, "Didn't you feel bad about this
> morning?" He said, "Are you crazy. I feel fine. Are you trying
> to start something?" I said, "No."*

In general the anger addict's attitude is, "How can I be doing
anything wrong when I feel so right?" Let Bella show us how it
works:

> *Bert agreed to go to a marriage counselor with me. At
> the counselor's he heard me say I felt hurt and fear when he
> yelled at me. After we left he yelled at me again, saying I'd at-
> tacked and blindsided him. I was confused. I didn't know what
> he meant or how he thought I had been attacking him.*

The accusatory nature of the abuser's angry outbursts usually leaves the partner wondering what she's "said wrong." It is not uncommon for the partner of an anger addict to mull over events, struggling to discover what she does or says that angers her mate. If he directs all his anger at her and blames her for it as well, if mutual friends tell her how lucky she is to have such a wonderful mate, if the abuse doesn't take place in public, if the abuser tells her he loves her, if her family of origin did not provide a good model of a loving relationship, she may have no idea that she is actually suffering from abuse. She will keep looking for rational reasons for her mate's behavior.

Abusive anger diminishes the partner's desire for sexual intimacy. When this occurs, the abuser then accuses *her* of being uncaring and unfeeling, and she may think that something is wrong with her.

Although the hostility stemming from the abuser's free-floating anger has nothing to do with the partner, it does affect her deeply. She will feel emotional pain even if she does not recognize that her mate is hostile towards her, and even if she thinks that she is to blame, in some as-yet-to-be-discovered way, for his anger.

Abusive anger may begin with irritable snaps and then evolve into rages. This increasing intensity and frequency usually develops very, very gradually over years, but it may develop very rapidly within the first year or months of the relationship. Two of the women I interviewed described a dramatic change in their mates' behavior which occurred right after marriage.

Although abusive anger is accusatory and blaming, the partner of the abuser does not provoke, nor does she consciously or unconsciously plan to provoke or "get" the abuser. On the contrary, as I listened to the partners and former partners of verbal abusers, I realized that they had made every effort to express themselves clearly and respectfully. Usually they felt that they had failed.

There are no particular phrases that identify abusive anger. To get a sense of what abusive anger sounds like, you might go back to the previous chapter and say all the abusive phrases listed there as angrily as you can. Or you might read them with your jaw clenched, spitting the words through your teeth. The greater impact they have when read angrily best demonstrates the impact they have on the partner.

Some signs of abusive anger are a lack of warmth from your mate as well as all verbal abuse, irritable outbursts, sneers, argumentativeness, temper tantrums, shouting, yelling, raging, explosiveness, and sarcasm that is directed toward you and/or others. Any one of these may signal to a woman that she is with an angry man. Robert Brownbridge, L.C.S.W., contributed the view, "Sarcasm is the tip of the iceberg which conceals a mountain of anger."

Physical signs of abusive anger include all the body language associated with anger, such as clenched teeth and a raised fist. Also, of course, any physical assault and destruction of your property is a demonstration of abusive anger.

Some verbal abusers do not express their anger overtly, but abuse much more covertly. These more covert abusers are also angry and hostile. However, they don't express their anger in the pattern of the anger addict. It seems that they may be more inclined to develop long-range plans to control and manipulate their partners.

Anger addicts, on the other hand, are usually quick to anger and are easily irritated. Most partners don't realize that an easily irritated person is an angry person. They believe instead that there are just some things their mate is sensitive to, but they just can't quite understand exactly what they are. In fact, the anger addict will reconstruct *whatever* he hears in such a way that it becomes for him the "reason" for venting his anger on his partner. The anger itself is irrational, as May discovered:

> At first I was concerned that I'd inadvertently anger him. Later, when I realized that there was no real reason for it, I was frightened of his irrationality.

CHAPTER X

Conditioning and the Partner

A scientist conducted an experiment. She put frog number one into a pan of very hot water. The frog jumped right out. Then she placed frog number two in a pan of cool water. This frog didn't jump out. Very gradually, the scientist raised the temperature of the water. The frog gradually adapted until it boiled to death.

— *Anonymous*

Part of conditioning is adapting. In other words, conditions may change around us and, like frog number two in the little story above, we may adapt very gradually. We are not inclined to notice gradual changes. This is how most partners adapt to verbal abuse. They slowly adapt until, like frog number two, they are living in an environment which is killing to their spirit.

Going back to our story, frog number one jumped right out of the hot water because she noticed a contrast between the comfortable air she had been in and the very hot water she was put into. She felt the difference. She was able to discriminate. If she had stayed in the hot water after experiencing that it was not a healthful environment, she would have been "denying" her experience, or acting unnaturally.

The partner is conditioned by her family of origin, by her culture, and by her relationship. None of us is entirely free from conditioning. Consequently, we adapt, and our conditioning influences the way we interpret our experience.

Since entire books have been written on cultural conditioning and on the inequalities in our society, this chapter will serve only as a brief review, focusing primarily on the factors which seem most to condition the partner not to recognize the abuse.

Primarily, the partner is conditioned to believe that her mate is rational toward her. This conditioning begins in early childhood. Who has not heard "You have nothing to cry about," said either to herself or to someone else. Even if a parent must refuse his child another piece of candy and the child cries, the child might be comforted: "I know you miss it and want it, yet I cannot give it to you." Thus the child learns early in her father's arms to grieve her losses rather than to believe that the irrational "You have nothing to cry about," is rational, real, and logical.

The partner is conditioned from early childhood not to trust her feelings and not to recognize the irrationality of verbal abuse. *All verbal abuse is irrational.* In the context of war, the rationality of which is questionable, there may be a certain rationality to a verbal attack. In the context of a relationship, verbal abuse is irrational, and the verbal abuser is behaving irrationally.

The partner's belief in the rationality of her mate is a primary assumption arising from and maintained by complex and diverse factors, not the least of which are her early childhood experiences.

Deep in her own psyche there is the conditioning of generations. C. G. Jung describes a patterning principle which organizes our thinking or way of perceiving as an archetype. The archetype or primary image of the masculine has been considered to be that of Logos, reason, or logic. Irrationality has been projected upon and identified with woman, the feminine. Consequently, the partner may believe that her mate is the rational one and that she is the irrational one in the relationship.

If the abuser denies his abusive behavior, saying it never happened or saying that what his partner has said or done is the *reason* for it, the partner may look for rationality, believing that her mate is logical. She may think, "There must be some reason he's angry at me," or "There must be some reason he thinks my work is not important," or "There must be some reason he thinks I am trying to start an argument."

The belief that her mate is behaving logically is one of the primary causes of the partner's confusion. He may hold the door for her at one moment, then scream at her when she answers a question the next moment. These rapid changes from rational to irrational behavior not only increase her confusion, but may also result in her increased determination to make some rational sense of it!

The partner is conditioned not only by her childhood caretakers and her culture, but also by the day-to-day abuse from her mate. Consequently, the partner may not only not recognize the abuse, but also may never in her life have asked the question, "Am I being verbally abused?" And she may never in her life have been asked the question, "Are you being verbally abused?" Many people don't really know what verbal abuse is. Usually it is a totally new concept to the partner. *When something is unnamed, and is seen by no one else, it has an aura of unreality about it.*

The verbal abuser especially undermines the partner's self-perception. If the partner is told with gradually increasing frequency that she is illogical, too sensitive, always trying to start an argument, competitive, always has to be right, etc., she may become conditioned to accept more and more abuse while experiencing more and more self-doubt. This conditioning is like brainwashing. It may extend beyond herself to her family, her interests, and her most cherished ideals. Consider the case of Lea:

> *Luke constantly presented to me that I had a flaky family. He did this in subtle ways. I gradually began to think he was in touch with the real world and I and my family weren't. I became confused. Actually, when I thought about my relatives, I realized they were highly respected and had made real contributions to society. Still I felt like there was something wrong with my background—like his family was more solid. Actually, now I can see that none of this was true. It was like brainwashing.*

Denise Winn, author of *The Manipulated Mind*, tells us that, with regard to brainwashing or psychological coercion, "social and psychological factors and unconscious conditions which combine to create it may each be powerful influencing forces on their own." She tells us that victims of brainwashing had certain experiences in common. Some of these are that "Their certainty was undermined . . . . Their behaviour was shaped by the use of rewards and other conditioning processes . . . . They were led to believe that no one at home cared what happened to them . . . . They felt out of control and learned helplessness . . . public humiliations served to undermine their egos . . . . Need for friendship and approval led them to comply . . . . Induced anxiety, guilt, fear and insecurity led to suggestibility . . . . The unpredictability of their captor's behaviour confused their expectations and assumptions.

113

Without a 'norm' to which they could adapt, they felt even less in control." (Winn, 1983, p. 35)

Winn also describes Robert Lifton's research. She tells us that "Lifton pinpointed the features which seemed to him to be characteristic of ideological totalism and necessary for maintenance of its hold over individuals." It is interesting to note that the first one named is "control over all forms of communication." (p. 21)

Certainly, within the relationship itself, the abuser can control all the interpersonal communication by denying the abuse and by refusing to discuss with his partner her pain and distress. As May put it:

> He has a secret agenda. He's trying to control you. If you don't know his secret, you're helpless.

In all cultures, words of wisdom and traditions are passed down from one generation to the next. This is part of our cultural heritage. Unfortunately, malevolent mores and half truths are also passed down to us. Many of these have become cliches through which the partner may interpret her experience. Some of these clichés and what they tell the partner are listed below.

MALEVOLENT MORES AND CLICHÉS

"It takes two." If the partner believes this, she will assume that she is to some extent to blame for the upset.

"Love conquers all." If the partner believes this, she may think that if she is more loving and accepting of her mate, he would reciprocate.

"You can rise above it." If the partner believes this, she may think that if she were just stronger she would be able to rise above her pain.

"Be glad you have a roof over your head." If the partner believes this, she may think she is expecting too much and should be glad for what she has.

"If you can't say something nice about someone, don't say anything at all." If the partner believes this, she may think it is disloyal or unkind or judgmental to talk to others about her mate's confusing behavior.

"A woman has to give a little more than a man." If the partner believes this, she may think that she should put forth more effort to understand her mate and to share herself with him so he'll understand her better.

"Be nice to people and they'll be nice to you." If the partner believes this, she may think that when her mate yells at her, he thought she wasn't being nice and that she can explain to him that she wasn't saying what he thought.

"Take it with a grain of salt." If the partner believes this, she may think that if she could take being yelled at more lightly, she wouldn't feel so badly.

"If you open up to him, he'll open up to you." If the partner believes this, she may think that if she shares herself, he'll share himself.

"Keep trying." If the partner believes this, she may think that there must be something she hasn't thought of that she could try in order to understand her mate and get him to understand her.

"Never give up." If the partner believes this, she may think that giving up the hope of reaching understanding with her mate is a failure on her part.

"His bark is worse than his bite." If the partner believes this, she may think that words shouldn't bother her.

"You can't expect too much." If the partner believes this, she may think that she should lower her expectations.

"People don't always mean what they say." If the partner believes this, she may think that no matter how badly she feels he didn't mean it, so she shouldn't feel it.

"Keep smiling." If the partner believes this, she may think that if she maintains her optimism, she'll discover a way to understand her mate.

"He doesn't know any better." If the partner believes this, she may think that if she explains what hurts her, he'll know better and stop hurting her.

"It's just a stage." If the partner believes this, she may think that if she waits, pretty soon he'll be in a better mood.

"Sticks and stones may break your bones, but words will never hurt you." If the partner believes this, she may think that no matter what he says, she shouldn't feel hurt.

"You should accept others the way they are." If the partner believes this, she may think that she should accept and understand her mate's behavior.

"Judge not, lest you be judged." The partner may fail to discriminate between acceptable and unacceptable behavior, thinking that to do so would be wrongly judgmental.

"You create your own reality." The partner may believe that she is doing something wrong—creating the difficulties in the relationship or the wrong feelings.

"Nobody said life was easy." The partner may believe that having difficulties in her relationship is the way life is and that her relationship is not any more difficult than anyone else's.

"For better or worse." If the partner believes this, she may think that better follows worse and that things will get better.

THE PARTNERS

The women I interviewed who were the partners and former partners of verbal abusers were primarily of middle and upper middle socioeconomic classes. Their levels of education ranged from high school graduate to Ph.D. Their occupations were varied and included artist, professor, homemaker, and shopkeeper. As partners of verbal abusers they had been:

Frustrated

Responsible

Hopeful

Empathetic

Compassionate

Naive

Trusting

Optimistic

Desirous of understanding

Tolerant

Accommodating

Confused

CHAPTER XI

The Recognition of Verbal Abuse and Asking for Change

Not to know is bad; not to wish to know is worse.
— *Nigerian Proverb*

When the partners of verbal abusers first begin to suspect that something is really wrong in their relationships, they usually describe some interaction with their mate to a counselor or confidante. Then they ask, "Is that normal?"

If the partner doesn't ask about the normalcy of her mate's behavior, she may, instead, ask if her friend has ever had such an experience as she has described. This first stage of recognition is the beginning of the partner's change from doubting herself to doubting her mate. It is a time when she is beginning to wonder if everyone's relationship has the kind of painful incidents that she experiences. It is a time when the partner does not yet realize that, in healthy relationships, one person doesn't yell at, put down, or hurt the other, and that, if any such infringement upon personal dignity does occur, it is an unusual and usually unprecedented event for which the perpetrator takes great pains to make amends.

When the partner begins to recognize verbal abuse for what it is, she has awakened from the illusion that her mate shares her reality. As she first glimpses her mate's reality, where dominance and Power Over substitute for Personal Power, she may find her mate's motivations nearly incomprehensible: it is hard to believe that he has treated her as he has in order to dominate and control

117

her, and not because there was anything wrong with her or her perceptions or her feelings or her thinking or her actions or her competence.

When the partner realizes that she and her mate are living and acting in different realities, she realizes that she is, in fact, being verbally abused. Since she experiences her power through mutuality and co-creation, this recognition *may be deeply shocking*. The partner's recognition of her mate's reality may be even more shocking, if he is successful in the world and *seemingly* powerful.

As shocking and painful as this recognition of the abuser's reality usually is, it is necessary because, otherwise, the partner may continue in the relationship for years hoping that her mate will understand what hurts her and that when he understands, it won't happen any more.

What happens if the partner cannot validate her own reality and recognize her mate's reality? If the partner does not recognize the abuser's reality, she will automatically fit his behavior into the context of her reality of mutuality and co-empowerment. Following is an analysis of an abusive incident which illustrates how this happens. This analysis describes the partner's and the abuser's thoughts and illustrates the difference between the abuser's and the partner's realities. Their thinking is common to many verbally abusive interactions in which there is a persecutor and a victim. I shall call this interaction The Shrimp Salad Drama. Have you experienced Shrimp Salad Dramas in your relationship?

At lunchtime the abuser comes into the kitchen asking, "Is there anything for lunch?"

"I left a shrimp salad in the refrigerator."

The abuser angrily yells, "What makes you think I want *salad*!"

The partner is thrown off balance. The anger and the implication that she is thinking he *wants* salad bring forth her response, "Why are you mad? I didn't say that."

"Just lay off of me. You're always trying to be right!"

They are in two different realities. The abuser is angry because his partner has protested with, "Why are you mad?" However, the partner thinks he is angry because she has somehow upset him by the way she mentioned the salad. After all, she "knows" he loves her. She believes that he must have felt that she was insisting on his having the salad but, actually, she'd be happy to have it for her own lunch and he just doesn't realize this. She thinks, "Maybe we can talk it out so he'll know I never meant he had to have the salad. (She thinks he is in her reality of mutuality.)

She explains, "I want you to know that what I meant was . . ."

She is now referring, of course, to her first statement that she'd left salad in the refrigerator. The abuser interrupts her because he is fighting her question, "Why are you mad?" He will take any response as adversarial because he does not want to acknowledge his irrational anger. He assumes that his partner is in his reality of Power Over. He thinks, "Aha! You are questioning me, trying to make me look bad, and trying to be right!"

Her attempt at reconciliation ("I want you to know that what I meant was . . .") is interrupted, with an angry, fed-up tone in the abuser's voice. He seems to be smoldering as he says, "If you're going to go on and on about it, I can eat out."

The abuser's total denial that he was abusive closes his mind to his partner. As he gets angrier, she tries harder to understand how saying the salad was in the refrigerator can make him think she thought he wanted it. He, of course, isn't angry about the salad. He's angry because he wants to vent his anger with complete impunity. This impunity was threatened when she said, "Why are you mad?" He felt that she was opposing him and that he might be losing his Power Over her.

The great tragedy in a verbally abusive relationship is that the partner's efforts to bring reconciliation, mutual understanding and intimacy are rejected out of hand by the abuser because to him they are adversarial. This is so because, if he isn't feeling Power Over his partner, he is feeling that she must be trying to overpower him. There is no mutuality in his reality.

Following are some more examples of how the partner may automatically fit the abuser and his behavior into her reality.

If her mate trivializes her work, the partner may believe that he really does want to support her and that he is only talking about it as unimportant because he doesn't realize how important it is to her, and as soon as he understands that it *is* important to her he will stop trivializing it. Here the partner fits what she's hearing together with her belief that her mate shares her reality and so wants to give her emotional support. Interestingly, abusers who trivialize their partners often brag about them to others as they would brag about a possession.

If he counters all her views, she may believe that he really respects her views but just can't accept the fact that she has them because he seems to think differently from her and so can't understand her. In this case, the partner fits what she hears from her mate into her reality of mutuality.

If he yells at her, she may believe that it is because he feels in some way hurt by something she said or did. She may also believe that he *wants* to know what she *really* said or did, so he'll know she really loves him and his hurt will be gone. In this way the partner fits what she is hearing into her reality of empathetic concern.

If he says he doesn't know what she's talking about, she may believe he wants very much to catch her meaning and to understand what she is talking about, so she must try harder to explain it more clearly. She is sure that her mate is striving to understand her and that he shares her reality of co-empowerment.

If he tells her she shouldn't feel what she's feeling, she may think that, since his intentions are really caring, she must have misheard what bothered her or, possibly, that her feelings are just wrong. If she fits his response into her reality, she can see no other reason why he would tell her that her feelings are wrong.

If he criticizes her words out of context, she may fit this criticism into her reality of mutuality by assuming that he is upset because he is trying very hard to follow her thinking but he can't unless she speaks with more accuracy or learns to understand how he thinks.

If he doesn't respond or talk to her, she may think he is very shy or slightly autistic, but really wants to communicate with her, since that is part of the joy of mutuality in a relationship. In this way the partner may fit a lack of response into her reality of mutuality.

If he says he cannot remember a conversation which she is absolutely certain he can remember, because it had been so disturbing, she may fit his inability to remember into her reality of mutuality by coming to the conclusion, as terrifying as it is, that he has a split personality. That is, sometimes he is in her reality and sometimes he's gone and an unfriendly voice takes over that he cannot remember. One partner harbored this fear of her mate's "split personality" for several months before she broached the subject with her counselor. When she did express her fear, she described her mate as having an autonomous voice that said things he didn't remember. If she believes that he sees the world as she does, that he shares her reality, it is easier for the partner to think her mate is crazy than to recognize that he is abusive.

One of the reasons the partner fits her mate's verbally abusive behavior into her reality of mutuality is that she, like many, is conditioned to see the world in terms of immediate cause and effect. For example she may believe, "If he is angry *at* me, then I must be the cause." However, the human psyche operates in a very different way. The cause of an event occurring today may be an event occurring many years before, in infancy or childhood. This is especially so with verbally abusive behavior. On the other hand, if her mate were not abusive and actually felt upset about something, he would, as any nonabusive person would, discuss the problem with his partner. He might say, for example, "I saw you spend time at the party talking to Joe. I thought you might rather be with him than with me, I felt lonely and jealous, so I would like to know how you feel about him and if I could have more time with you at parties."

Even if he finds it difficult to define his own feelings and thus does not realize that he is jealous, he will at least know that he is unhappy and needs to talk with his partner.

Recognizing the abuser's reality helps the partner to recognize the abuse for what it is. When she no longer sees her mate's behavior from an immediate cause-and-effect standpoint, the partner might realize, "Oh, he yelled at me because he wants to control or intimidate me, not because of something I've said or done." Or "He said that to put me down so he can feel powerful. I will not accept this abuse."

Here is another way that the partner's inability to recognize her mate's reality may affect her ability to recognize verbal abuse. Because she thinks that her mate shares her reality of mutuality, Reality II, she "knows" he is striving to understand her. Consequently, she may think that she's just not good at explaining herself or getting across to her mate what she really means. Otherwise, he wouldn't get angry. Consequently, she doesn't see the disrespect for what it is. Her ability to discriminate is impaired. To discriminate means to "see the difference." If the partner can see the difference between her reality and her mate's, she can discriminate.

"How can I know that it's not something I've said or done in some unconscious way that makes him mad?" many partners ask. These partners do not yet have Reality II self-esteem. A partner with Reality II self-esteem would not ask this question, because she knows that there is *no* justification for being yelled at or snapped at.

Many partners live with their mates for many years before coming to the realization that they do not share the same reality. Knowing that there is nothing wrong with her and that the abuse is irrational does not necessarily lessen the partner's pain. On the contrary, the abuse is not only painful, but now may also be more frightening to the partner because she realizes that it is irrational. We naturally fear the irrational because acts of violence and abuse are irrational and are irrationally denied or justified by the perpetrators. One of the reasons that it is important to recognize verbal abuse is that it is a warning sign that physical abuse may eventually erupt.

BASIC RIGHTS IN A RELATIONSHIP

Besides understanding the various categories of verbal abuse and recognizing the abuser's reality, it is useful to understand the basic rights of relationship which are violated by verbal abuse. Following is a list of some of these rights:

The right to goodwill from the other.

The right to emotional support.

The right to be heard by the other and to be responded to with courtesy.

The right to have your own view, even if your mate has a different view.

The right to have your feelings and experience acknowledged as real.

The right to receive a sincere apology for any jokes you find offensive.

The right to clear and informative answers to questions that concern what is legitimately your business.

The right to live free from accusation and blame.

The right to live free from criticism and judgment.

The right to have your work and your interests spoken of with respect.

The right to encouragement.

The right to live free from emotional and physical threat.

The right to live free from angry outbursts and rage.

The right to be called by no name that devalues you.

The right to be respectfully asked rather than ordered.

You need to feel safe and respected within your relationship. I believe that, if there is respect and goodwill in a relationship, other issues can be addressed. However, until the issue of verbal abuse and the abuser's underlying need for Power Over is resolved, little progress, if any, can be made in the relationship. That is to say, if there is *no* verbal abuse there *is* openness and a willingness to discuss the hopes, fears, desires, needs, and expectations of both parties.

I do not believe that two people in two different realities can develop a relationship, although they may live in the illusion of one. Just as the partner has perceived the abuser's reality, so too must the abuser recognize his own reality and his own behavior and come to terms with his own sense of Personal Powerlessness.

Now, if you were to realize that you and your mate are in different realities and that he was saying some things to you that were abusive, and if at the same time you were to realize that he was saying these things because he really felt powerless inside, it would not be a good idea to think that you could explain this to him. In fact, to try to do so would put you right back into being subject to more abuse because he would see your "explanation" as a defense. You would be stepping into his reality, where a defense is met with a greater attack.

"What can I do, then?" you might ask in despair. There is something you can do. There are steps you can take to protect yourself and to determine whether or not your mate is willing and able to change, whether he wants to change, and whether there is a possibility of connection and intimacy in your relationship. If you are in a new relationship, you may choose to leave the relationship immediately. However, if you have no job, have dependent children, feel fear, or lack self-confidence, you may need time to decide what to do. In the meantime, you can decide what you will and what you will not accept from your mate and you can inform him of your decisions. In making these decisions, you must rely upon your own feelings and your own judgment—the very feelings and judgment you have been conditioned by the abuse to doubt and to fear acting upon.

In order to implement these steps, you will need to act at your own pace. In most cases, it is very beneficial to get support from professional counseling, support groups, and friends.

If you are in an abusive relationship, there are a number of issues you may need to consider. You may need to evaluate what does and does not work for you in your relationship, as well as your emotional and financial dependency. You may need to become aware of your unmet needs for connection and intimacy and your right to be treated with courtesy, respect, dignity, and empathy.

Setting limits and asking for change is very difficult and challenging. Once you recognize your needs and rights and begin to ask for change, you confront the possibility that no change will be forthcoming. Asking for change is important, however, for only by doing so will you discover whether or not the possibility of a healthful relationship exists with your mate. If your mate is a confirmed verbal abuser, when you start setting limits and asking for change, he may increase the intensity of the abuse in an attempt to increase his control over you.

If it has taken you some time to recognize the abuse for what it is and to recognize the abuser's reality, it is likely that your mate will take some time also to recognize your reality and to admit to what he is doing. Keep in mind that not all abusers will change. After all, they are not suffering in the way that their partners are suffering. Consequently, they are not motivated to the degree that their partners are. Be aware that unless an abuser is willing to give up his denial of the abuse, he cannot begin to change. *In order to change, to develop empathy and understanding, to become nonabusive, he will need to work through all that has engendered within him his deep feelings of Personal Powerlessness.*

You do not need to accept your mate's behavior. With support and counseling, you can determine your needs. You can set limits and you can ask for change. It takes time to fully realize what has been happening in your relationship and how the abuse has affected you, especially if the abuse has been severe.

How severe is the abuse? Partners who have been subject to all the categories of verbal abuse have been severely abused. If you are with an anger addict, you have been severely abused. If you feel unexpected stabs of pain from what you hear from your mate, you have been severely abused. If you have never felt a sense of understanding and resolution after talking over a hurtful incident with your mate, you have been severely abused. If you have been with a verbal abuser for a number of years, you have been severely abused. As was stated in the introduction, the intensity of anguish which the victim suffers determines the extent of the injury. The quality of the experience of the victim defines the degree of abuse.

I have found that verbal abuse affects the partner's sense of herself and her self-esteem, usually without her recognizing it.

Therefore, as might be expected, the process of recognizing verbal abuse includes the process of recovering from the abuse. Recovery is addressed in the next chapter.

If you suffer from verbal abuse in your relationship, or suspect that you do, these are some steps you can take:

1. *Get professional counseling support.* Find a supportive counselor who is experienced with the issue of verbal abuse and with whom you feel comfortable. Sources include referrals from therapists in other fields, BWA (Battered Women's Alternatives) recommendations, referrals from social-service agencies, and referrals from friends.

2. *Ask your mate to go to this counselor with you.* Firmly and clearly tell your mate that in order to have a happier and more satisfying relationship, you want him to see a counselor with you. If he is unwilling or this seems impossible to you, go by yourself. You will already have met and chosen the counselor you want to work with. In the counseling relationship you will gain much needed support and clarity.

3. *Start setting limits.* Stating what you will and what you will not accept from your mate and informing him of your decisions is called setting limits. By firmly setting limits and calling the abuser on every abuse, you may bring to his attention the fact that he is being abusive. However, it is also possible that he may refuse to hear anything you say and continue to abuse you.

   Setting limits may be very difficult because, of course, you do not know whether or not your mate can or will honor your limits, nor do you know whether or not he will *want* to honor your limits. You do not know whether he will tell you that he will try to honor your limits or whether he will tell you that he can say anything he wants. You do not know whether he simply has a few bad habits or whether he is really hostile. Setting limits is a serious proposition because, when you are setting limits, you are not threatening. Threats are often idle forms of manipulation. Threats are stated in the form "If you . . . I'll . . ." Setting a limit is stating a fact: "I will not accept . . ."

   When you set limits you speak from your own Personal Power, and you speak for the spirit of life at your center. You decide what is harmful and what is nourishing to your spirit.

In order to set limits, you need to know what your limits are. This means that you, and only you, must decide what you will and will not accept in your relationship. This is when the *extraordinary* self-esteem I have described throughout this book must be called upon. This self-esteem is available to you because it arises from the spirit of life at your center.

When you are ready with your self-esteem and your trust in yourself, you are ready to set limits. To do so is to simply say: "I will not accept . . ." It is up to you to choose, from the fifteen categories of verbal abuse, the one you want to start with. For example, "I will not accept comments or 'jokes' which diminish or disparage me or put me down."

It isn't easy for the partner of a verbal abuser to set limits because she must give up all her usual ways of seeking resolution and reconciliation—ways which she has tried during all the upsetting experiences she has had with her mate. These ways include explaining, trying to understand, trying harder to be understood, trying to figure out what went wrong, and so forth.

Besides self-esteem, setting limits requires extraordinary trust in yourself and your own feelings and your own perceptions—so much trust that if you are, for example, yelled at, *you know* that:

Even if he thinks it is justified, you will not accept it.

Even if he thinks it is a joke, you will not accept it.

Even if he does not understand, you will not accept it.

Even if he says it is your fault, you will not accept it.

Even if he says you do not know what you're talking about, you will not accept it.

Even if he says you are just trying to be right, you will not accept it.

Even if he says you are a bitch, you will not accept it.

Even if he says a hundred things, you will not accept it, *nor will you accept the hundred things.*

Even if you have made a mistake you will not accept the abuse. You know, for example, that you will not accept being put down or raged at for a simple mistake.

With Reality II self-esteem, you know that you do not deserve to be yelled at. With Reality II self-esteem, you know that *you do not deserve any verbal abuse at all.*

4. *Stay in the present, trying to dwell neither on the past nor on your concerns for the future.* Become aware in the present, moment by moment, of any angry outburst or disparagement directed at you. With this awareness you will need to respond to the abuse in a new way. In the past you may have told your mate when you were upset, hurt, frustrated, etc. You may have told him what you were upset about, and you may have asked him not to yell at you, or you may have asked him to check with you to find out what you really were saying before he got mad. You also may have found that none of this was effective in stopping the abuse.

Your goal is to call the abuser on every offense. Once you have determined your limits, you reinforce them by calling a halt to every bit of abuse you hear. Specific responses to each category of abuse are suggested in the next chapter. At any time, however, a firm, authoritative "Stop it!" is effective.

Your authoritative response will give your mate the clear message that you mean what you say and will not tolerate any abuse. You will need to respond as soon as you hear the tone of his voice. If you become caught by the words you will simply become confused, as did the partner in the "Shrimp Salad Drama" example above.

Remember: any response such as "What I meant was . . ." suggests to the abuser that his reality is valid—that you are the adversary and that he can step up his attacks, even claiming that you are attacking him. Of course he is not justified, but he will take any explanation as adversarial and defensive.

5. *Be aware that you can leave any abusive situation.* Please note that four of the forty women I interviewed had been hit by their mates. Most had been repeatedly yelled at, most had at one time or another thought they were about to be hit.

Most said, "he's never hit me, but I have been afraid of his anger."

Carry enough money with you so that you can pay for transportation home from wherever you are. You are a free citizen. You never have to stay where you feel uncomfortable. Carry your personal phone book with you so that you have the numbers of friends if you need to call someone. If you are out at a party or a restaurant, or staying in a hotel and you are being yelled at, put down, etc., and you find that saying "Stop it" does not put an end to the abuse, or if for any reason you do not feel comfortable remaining, simply leave. This is your right and your responsibility to yourself.

Keep a bag packed in your car, if you have your own car, or else in a safe and easily available place so that you know that you do not have to stay where you are subject to any kind of abuse. Plan ahead where and how you will go if you need to leave your residence.

These steps will give you a sense of control over your own life and help to alleviate the fear of being hurt one more time.

6. *Ask for changes that you want in your relationship.* Intimacy in a relationship requires a *mutual* intention to communicate, to understand, to respond appropriately, as well as the intention to support the other emotionally.

Setting limits is a way of asking for change. You may also ask your mate to discuss with you other changes you may desire. These may include the negotiation of the following:

How much time you need to yourself and how much time you would like to spend together.

Setting aside a special time each week to discuss current issues in the relationship.

Making plans together for the future.

How to jointly manage finances.

SOME DIFFICULTIES YOU MAY ENCOUNTER

If you have been blamed for abuse, you may feel somehow guilty or at fault or as if you are betraying your mate by discussing your concerns about your relationship with an outside party. You may even feel that reading about verbal abuse may harm your relationship. You may have these feelings if you have been conditioned to believe that your difficulties and pain are your fault.

You may also be conditioned to feel wrong about setting limits and refusing to accept abuse. For example, phrases such as "You're just looking for trouble" or "You're always trying to start something" may condition you to believe that the abuse is "your fault" and that you are making things worse.

If you are with a verbal abuser and are resolved to set limits and to challenge your mate on any infringement, you may continue to meet with intense denial. In this case, remember that a verbal abuser defines his partner and the interpersonal reality. He also defines himself, particularly that he is right and nonabusive. It is important, therefore, that you completely accept your own perceptions and your own feelings. When you can define your own reality as separate and different from your mate's, you gain clarity, self-esteem, and autonomy.

Knowing that what the abuser has told you about yourself is not at all true but is, in fact, abusive, can help you to recognize how your mate has attempted to define you in terms of his reality. One way to become more aware is to turn each accusatory statement around into an "I know that I am *not*" statement. Following are some examples:

I know that I am *not* competitive.

I know that I am *not* always trying to start a fight.

I know that I am *not* too sensitive.

I know that I am *not* a bitch.

I know that I am *not* selfish.

I know that I am *not* judgmental.

I know that I am *not* attacking.

I know that I am *not* trying to have the last word.

I know that I am *not* [keep adding everything you have been told you are, because if you are with a verbal abuser, you can be certain that you are not what you've been told.]

Another difficulty may occur if the abuse has taken place primarily when no one else was around and was then denied by the abuser. Since this abuse occurs in secret, no one in the world can validate your experience. You may think you have taken everything wrong as you have so often been told you do. You may truly think there *is* something wrong with you because no one else was around to say "Hey! that's abusive." Or you may think your mate has no idea of what he's doing.

If this is the case, it is important to remember that most crimes *are* committed in secret just like most verbal abuse. Just as the rapist knows what he is doing in secret, *the abuser knows what he is doing in secret.* He may not know what compels him. The confirmed verbal abuser can be counted on to deny the abuse vehemently and to tell his partner angrily that her perceptions are wrong or that she is responsible for the abuse.

If the abuser continues to deny the abuse, then his denial locks him into a more-or-less permanent psychological stance. The abuser who denies all, is unwilling to discuss the issue, and remains hostile does not want to change. In order to change, he would have to break though his denial, admit to the abuse, and work through the issues which left him with such a great need for dominance and Power Over.

Another real difficulty the partner may encounter is the painful realization that she is the primary and often the only person he abuses. "Why would he do this to me?" she might ask. The psychological reasons that this abuse occurs most frequently in relationships are discussed in Chapter XV and have to do with the psychological phenomena of projection.

Knowledge of the abuser's reality brings the partner an opportunity for real growth and inner peace. She can discover through confrontation and counseling whether or not the abuser wants to change. She can cherish and accept herself and build her Reality II self-esteem. She can choose a more nourishing environment.

"My peace of mind is worth everything I went through," said Bella.

Recognizing verbal abuse for what it is, is emotionally painful. It has to do with loss—the loss of illusion—and grieving that loss. This pain runs its course and makes room for the natural healing process. It isn't insidious and damaging the way the pain of abuse is. As Ann put it,

I realize I kept forgetting the hurt and pain, and from what I've read I know I was beginning to show the symptoms of a battered wife. I'm shocked.

Cora summed it up this way:

It is incredibly painful and heartbreaking when you realize that the man you love is hostile toward you.

Clearly, verbal abuse is hurtful to the spirit. Nevertheless, through knowledge, awareness, and action we may heal the spirit. In doing so we must face the fact that psychological freedoms are usually won through emotional pain and feelings of loss. None have been won anywhere and in any time without effort and action. Even a plant seeks light and the most nourishing environment in which to grow. The survivor of abuse can do no less.

Lastly, be aware that there is nothing you can say or do to change another person. The other person must want to change for the sake of the relationship. You cannot teach another by explaining or telling how you feel or what you want to hear. You can only set your limits and ask for change.

If the partner recognizes that her mate is living in Reality I, and that he is unwilling or unable to change, she will face the loss of her hope for his companionship, partnership, love, and acceptance. She must decide if she needs to remove herself from the abusive relationship and how she can best protect and nourish herself and the spirit of life at her center.

Only one of the women I interviewed, a very attractive and articulate sixty-three-year-old, consciously chose to remain in a verbally abusive relationship. Following is an excerpt from that interview:

"I am married to a verbal abuser."
"How long have you been married to him?"
"Forty-two years."
"When did you recognize that you were being verbally abused?"
"After about thirty years."
"And you decided to stay in the relationship?"
"Yes. But I think I chose the hardest path."

CHAPTER XII

Responding with Impact to Verbal Abuse

> I got so used to hearing what I was always hearing,
> that after a while I stopped hearing what I was al-
> ways hearing. Do you know what I mean?
> — *A Partner*

This chapter suggests specific responses to each of the categories of verbal abuse which were described in Chapter VIII. Each specific response enforces the limits you have set. For example: If your limit is, "I won't tolerate being snapped at or yelled at," your enforcement is, "*Stop it!*"

If you are experiencing some verbal abuse in your relationship, you may wish to move ahead to specific responses. However, in order to be more effective, I recommend that you read this introductory section on boundaries, possibilities for success, and general guidelines for responding to abuse. The more you understand why certain responses are particularly effective, the more able you will be to enforce your limits.

When you set limits, you establish your boundaries. Your boundaries help to protect your integrity as an individual. They help to define you. All verbal abuse violates your boundaries in some way. If you are verbally abused, it is important that you respond with an awareness of the violation that has occurred. *Responding appropriately enforces your limits and reestablishes or confirms your boundaries.* Following are several examples of how verbal abuse violates your boundaries.

If you are completely ignored by your mate, if he looks right through you as if you didn't exist, your boundaries are being violated. This is so because you are being treated as if your individuality does not exist, as if you have no boundary to set you off from the background scenery. This is a violation. We do not usually think of ourselves as having boundaries, but it is helpful to do so. Actually, boundary violation *is* the experience of abuse.

Here is a second example of how verbal abuse violates the victim's boundaries: If you are called names, your boundaries are violated. You are being defined by the abuser in his terms, not yours. It is as if *your* boundaries which establish and define your individuality do not exist. This is a violation.

Take a moment now to imagine being ordered by your mate to do something. Can you tell how being ordered violates your boundaries? When you are ordered to do something, you are being treated as if you are not a separate individual to be consulted or asked. You are being treated as if you had no boundary—nothing to separate you from the abuser—as if you were his extension—an instrument of his will. This is a great invasion of your boundaries and a violation of your personhood.

Denial is also a violation of your boundaries. If your experience is denied or discounted, the abuser has invaded your boundaries. He has moved through them as if to enter your mind, and then has claimed to know what your experience actually was. Generally, according to him, it was a fantasy. In so many words, "You don't know what you're talking about." This terrible invasion is, of course, a violation.

These examples suggest the importance of responding to verbal abuse in a way that reestablishes and reconfirms your boundaries.

Verbal abuse is a violation, not a conflict. There is a definite difference between conflict and abuse. In a conflict each participant wants something different. In order to resolve the conflict, the two people in the relationship discuss their wants, needs, and reasons while mutually seeking a creative solution. There may or may not be a solution, but no one forces, dominates, or controls the other.

Verbal abuse, on the other hand, is very different from a conflict. If we describe verbal abuse from the standpoint of boundary violation, we would describe it as an intrusion upon, or disregard of, one's self by a person who disregards boundaries in a sometimes relentless pursuit of Power Over, superiority, and dominance by covert or overt means.

If you have encountered verbal abuse to which you wish to respond, you may find it helpful to take a few minutes to evaluate your relationship. What are the possibilities for improvement? Following are some questions which may help you to evaluate the quality of your relationship:

Does your mate enrich your life?

Does he bring you joy?

Do you feel a real connection to him?

Do you think in the same way and share the same dreams?

Does he show goodwill?

Good will in a relationship is a warmth and honesty which comes from one's deepest sense of truth. It is a concern for the other's well-being as well as a strong desire to understand the other. It is demonstrated by a movement toward the other (in a psychological sense) with the intention of reaching mutual understanding and respect.

Although you may experience some verbal abuse, if your mate shows goodwill and you can answer "yes" to the above questions, there is a good chance he fits into the category of "having some misbehaviors" which he may give up when you enforce your limits.

If you are in a brand-new relationship and see warning signs of verbal abuse, you may be wise to let the relationship go. It is not likely that a man who needs to dominate and control or to find a scapegoat for his anger will change easily, if at all. This is especially so in a new relationship in which he has invested little time and energy. It is also likely that when the newness wears off he will become more abusive. On the other hand, if he is thoughtlessly trying out a few misbehaviors he's learned in the past, he may change quickly when he knows you've spotted them and won't tolerate them.

If you are in a long-term relationship and are experiencing verbal abuse, if the relationship is important to you, and if you decide to respond to the abuse as this chapter suggests, you will soon discover for yourself whether or not your mate will stop his abusive behavior. You will also gain awareness and self-esteem in the process.

The responses suggested in this chapter are designed to make an impact that stops the abuser, enforces the partner's boundaries, and protects her from further abuse. These responses may enable the abuser to recognize what he is doing, realize that he can't keep doing it, and stop the abuse.

If you have been verbally abused in your relationship, you may have discovered that explaining and trying to understand have not improved your relationship. Therefore, I recommend that you respond in a new way—a way that will make an emotional, psychological, and intellectual impact upon your mate.

He *may* change when he finds that you *do* know when you are being abused, that you *have* set limits, that you *mean* what you say, and that you *will not take* behavior you don't like, even if he says, "You don't know what you're talking about!"

Please do not, however, blame yourself if you cannot make an impact. If your mate won't or can't change, you may need to end the relationship.

To begin, here are some recommendations: Tell your mate that you will not be responding to him in the usual way. Write him a letter, if that is easier. Also, tell him that you haven't been happy with some of the things you've heard from him; that you want to have a really good relationship with him; that you would like to see some changes in communication; that in the past you have tried to explain to him what bothered you about some of his behaviors; and that you don't feel that you have been successful. Assure him that you will be letting him know what you want and what you don't want in your relationship, that you have limits, and that you will let him know immediately if he oversteps them. Ask him for his cooperation.

He may not believe that any changes are necessary. If this is so, it is because he is not suffering abuse. He may say, "you are making problems" or "you are trying to ruin the relationship." If he does, tell him, "Stop it right now! No more accusations!"

He may deny or seem blind to the fact that he is really abusive. However, you may still make an impact upon him with your responses. These responses are designed to awaken your mate to the fact that his behavior is *inappropriate* and is *unacceptable to you*. Some people change their behavior when they experience the impact of a strong response. Others are very resistant to change.

If your mate remains abusive, it is not your fault, nor is it your responsibility. By taking these steps you will know that you can recognize verbal abuse when it is occurring and that you can respond appropriately—no small task.

If you are often too stunned, caught too much off guard, too shocked, or in too much pain or confusion to respond to verbal abuse with even a "Stop it," you may be in an extremely toxic and unhealthy relationship. Do get support. If you don't know where to turn, follow the suggestions in Chapter XIII on recovery.

To respond with strength, it is important to know (besides knowing how and when your boundaries are violated) that verbal abuse may be a sign of emotional immaturity. Not knowing this, partners sometimes respond to childish outbursts such as temper tantrums and "nasty" name calling as if they were coming from a *rational* adult. For instance, when some partners are called names they wonder, "What am I doing that's making him think that of me." Of course, he isn't abused for what she *does*.

A child's name calling ("You poo poo!") and an adult's name calling ("You bitch!") both originate within the same level of emotional development. The child hasn't had time to mature, so we are not disturbed by his name calling. The adult who is still name calling not only is disturbing but may also be dangerous.

Countering is another example of immaturity. For instance, if you have been around a four-year-old who is striving to learn how things are, you will probably have heard countering: "It's not that way," "You're wrong."

To the four-year-old, his view is the only view. The child wants the world to be fixed and sure. The mature adult recognizes that it isn't—that there are as many points of view as there are people.

Through the process of maturation we not only learn to respect other people's views and perspectives, but we also learn how to express anger appropriately. For the most part, we take after our own parents in the expression of anger. Knowingly or unknowingly, parents teach through example. By the time we reach adulthood we have learned how to express anger appropriately. The abuser has missed this crucial learning. And this, by the way, is exactly why he is angry and abusive.

Anger properly expressed is not abusive, destructive, blaming, or accusatory. On the other hand, when anger is expressed abusively, it is destructive and hurtful. Anger *can* be expressed in a healthy way. For example, when the partner responds to abuse with a forceful "Stop that!" she uses her anger to protect herself. This constructive use of anger is quite different from destructive blame and accusation. Destructive blame ("You know what you did!") and accusation ("You're just trying to get out of it!") are forms of abusive anger. One might imagine how confusing this abuse can be to the partner who may have heard it throughout her life.

A WORD OF CAUTION: *If you are feeling stunned, shocked, or in too much pain to speak, if your mate seems to go out of control with anger; if you are feeling fearful of him, if he has threatened you with any harm, if he has hit you or threatened to hit or hurt you, you should not be dealing with his abusive behavior alone and you must question the health of staying around him.*

Responding to verbal abuse means responding with strength so as to make an impact. It is not easy, so go at your own pace. You are not involved in word games when you are living with abuse. You are fighting for your spirit, your sanity, your soul.

When you are caught off guard, it is difficult to think of what to say. It is easier to remain calm around an abusive *stranger*, such as the driver who cusses you out as he passes you, than it is to stay calm around an abusive mate. This is so for many reasons—one being that your "heart is open" to your mate and he has, therefore, the power to reject you. Abuse is rejection. It is painful and toxic.

A final caution: Don't ever delude yourself into thinking that you should have the ability to stay serene no matter how you are treated. Your serenity comes from the knowledge that you have a fundamental right to a nurturing environment and a fundamental right to affirm your boundaries.

If you are experiencing verbal abuse and want to respond as authoritatively as possible, before you begin trying some of these suggestions, I recommend that you read the rest of this book. Then, review the responses. The more you know about verbal abuse and the abusive personality, the more able you will be to respond with strength and impact.

At first it may be helpful to practice role-playing with a friend or counselor. This way your friend can read the abusive statements from Chapter VIII and you can practice appropriate responses. If you don't have someone to practice with, put an empty chair in front of you and imagine the abuser sitting across from you. Then, try playing both roles, speaking out loud if possible. This role-playing affords you the opportunity of gaining insights into the kinds of abuse you have experienced.

Besides role-playing, it might be helpful to you to review the list of categories of verbal abuse in Chapter VIII to discover whether you can give one or two examples for each category. This will help you to recognize abuse when you hear it.

WHEN YOU RESPOND TO VERBAL ABUSE

❑ Know that when you are being put down, ordered around, yelled at, and so forth, you are being abused. And abuse is unjust, disabling, and destructive.

❑ Remember that the abuser is not speaking in a rational, adult way.

❑ Know that you are responding to a person who is in some way trying to control, dominate, or establish superiority over you.

❑ Know that you have done nothing to cause it.

❑ Know that it is not healthy to live in an abusive atmosphere.

❑ Distance yourself from the abuser by seeing his immaturity for what it is.

❑ Respond with a tone of authority and firmness that shows that you mean business, are serious, and will not tolerate any more abuse.

❑ Stay aware. Concentrate on the *present*. Notice what *your* senses tell you. How do *you* feel? How does he sound to *you*? What do *you* see?

In general, when you respond to verbal abuse, speak firmly and clearly, stand or sit straight and tall, hold your head high, look the abuser in the eye, and breathe deeply, letting your abdomen expand with the intake of air.

Learning to recognize and respond to verbal abuse takes time, energy, effort, determination, and dedication. Even after your mate stops shouting at you or putting you down or indulging in whatever had been his abusive behavior, there are factors in your relationship that may need work. If he is willing to work with you, if he wants to change, if he has goodwill toward you, if he has been able to acknowledge his abusive behavior and to ask you what you want and need in the relationship, then you both may be able to build a fine relationship.

How soon can you expect results—no more abuse? Much depends upon your mate. You can't "make it happen" all by yourself. For example, if he cannot or will not stop yelling at you even when you tell him to "Stop!" and if he is determined that you cause his anger, you cannot expect results. If he does not want to change, then, of course, he won't. In general, you will know within a month or two whether he is changing because he will either have stopped abusing you or he will be continuing to abuse you.

If he is deeply concerned about you and cares about your well-being and if he wants a healthy relationship with you, you may see results in the first week.

Suggested responses to each of the categories of verbal abuse follow. Each category is described in depth in Chapter VIII. You do not need to memorize all the suggested responses. You might convey the same meaning in your own words.

RESPONSES TO SPECIFIC CATEGORIES OF ABUSE

If you are in an extremely difficult situation and need a quick, all-purpose response to verbal abuse which will see you through most verbally battering situations try, "Stop that kind of talk right now!"

Responding to Withholding

Withholding is a purposeful silent treatment and, as explained earlier, it is a violation of your boundaries. You need no longer sit through long hours of silence punctuated by *your* occasional questions, comments on the news of the day, or expressions of personal interest while you get no response from your mate. Whether you are out to dinner, at home or spending a holiday at the beach, if you have experienced hours, or days, or whatever is your limit of nonresponsive closed silence, leave the area stating firmly, clearly, and matter-of-factly as you leave, "I am feeling very bored with your company."

Then be gone as long as you want to. You may, or may not, make an impact, but at least you won't be bored. Reading a book or taking your children out for ice cream is less boring and less painful than hoping for a response and getting the "silent treatment."

Alternatively, one woman put on her earphones and sat down to dinner with a favorite tape playing. She gestured and hummed through dinner to music only she could hear. Her unusual behavior made an impact on her mate. He soon made overtures to engage her in conversation.

Responding to Countering

If your mate counters your ideas, feelings, and perceptions, or goes so far as to refute what he misconstrues you to have said, you may in either case say authoritatively and decisively, "Stop!" while holding your arm out in front of you at a right angle to your body, palm out, facing him, in the style of a traffic officer. Follow the word "Stop!" with the request: "Please look at my lips." Then repeat your original statement while speaking slowly and distinctly.

Do *not* explain what you said or what you meant because a "counterer" will simply counter your explanation. Repeat this process every time you are countered. (Remember, you *have* a right to your own thoughts and perceptions.) If you stay aware and alert and *stop* countering on every occasion, you may affect your mate's behavior to the extent that he stops countering you.

If you express your view of something and he says, "Oh, I don't see it that way," that is fine. He isn't countering you. He is simply stating that he has a different view.

In the lampshade dialogue in Chapter VIII, the abuser countered his own statements when they were repeated back to him. If your mate expresses an opinion to you and you repeat it back to him to express your understanding and then he counters your repeat of his statement, stop everything right there! Do not try to express understanding of his second statement. Recognize with your increased awareness and trust in yourself that *your original understanding of him was correct*. He is countering you, not trying to reach understanding with you. Knowing this, simply say, "Hold it! I'm not following you. Would you please write that down" or "Cut it out!" or "Stop countering me!"

If he refuses, don't spend even a minute trying to understand what he is saying, and don't take him seriously. He isn't struggling to be understood or to understand you. If you try to understand a counterer's meaning, you will become confused and frustrated.

Another response to countering that works in most situations is "So you say," said very calmly, slowly and emphatically. It is undebatable and leaves the counterer with full responsibility for his own statement while leaving you with the right to your own opinion.

Sometimes countering comes in the form of a challenge. If after expressing a personal perception such as "I thought the play was great," you hear a challenge such as "You can't prove it," the way to respond is to simply say, "No."

Then disengage. Leave the room. You might take a walk, visit a friend, take yourself to lunch, go to the library, check out the powder room, window shop, or take the children to the park.

You have a right to your own view, your own opinion, and your own perspective. There may be as many views of something as there are people on the planet. Each one's view fits with her or his perspective, experience, beliefs, and so forth. When you are told that your view is wrong, it is as though someone has stepped into your body and mind and then negated your experience. Clearly, countering is a violation of your boundaries.

Responding to Discounting

Discounting is a very troublesome form of abuse. How do you respond to discounting? It seems the damage is done—you are put down and hurt by a darting jab. Then, when you protest with, "Why did you say that?" or "That's not true!" or "I feel bad; that wasn't very nice," you are told that your experience does not count. It counts for nothing. It is discounted with, "You're jumping to conclusions!" or "You're blowing everything out of proportion!" This is a tremendous violation and invasion of your boundaries; it is as if the abuser has taken up residence in your mind and swept out your experience, replacing it with his own ideas.

Don't try to understand how your mate can think that or say that. Don't try to get him to understand that you *don't* jump to conclusions or that you *aren't* blowing it out of proportion. Don't protest with, "Why did you say that?" Respond with natural outrage if for no other reason than that *you* don't like it, period.

What will make an impact? Try, "Stop that kind of talk right now!" or "Hold it! I don't ever want to hear that kind of talk from you!" or "Cut it out!"

These responses may be opposed by a confirmed abuser. However, they are not easily discounted. Use them any time you encounter verbal abuse and are caught by surprise.

If you are more perplexed than outraged when you hear discounting such as, "You don't know what you're talking about!" respond very forcefully as if you've made a great discovery, throwing your hands up into the air while exclaiming "Aha! So *that's* what you believe!" This works with many "you" statements. If he says "yes," simply say, with great meaning and mystery, "I see."

The one thing the abuser tries to avoid is taking responsibility for what he says. This response lets him know that you hold him responsible and know that his beliefs are not your beliefs.

Responding to Abuse Disguised as a Joke

When you are put down and you tell your mate that you didn't like what he said and he tells you it was "just a joke," or when he laughs uproariously about it, you have suffered from abuse disguised as a joke. In order to respond to this form of abuse, it is helpful to know that he has put you down because he thinks doing so will put him up, so to speak. (This says something about his rationality and his maturity.)

In some cases, when the partner tells her mate that she didn't like what he said, he may take this self-revelation as an attack, and instead of apologizing and expressing sympathy for her feelings, he may put her down again by telling her, "You don't have a sense of humor."

If your hear this from your mate, *do* realize that he has violated your boundaries and invaded your being and has presumed to define the most intimate quality of your nature—your sense of humor. *Don't* try to explain to him what wasn't funny about the joke. Don't try to explain to him the kinds of jokes you find humorous. Don't try to explain to him the kinds of jokes that, for some reason which you aren't aware of, you don't find humorous and would like him please not to say to you. Don't ask him what he meant or why he said it. Don't spend time wondering if he understood how it sounded *even if he's acting like it sounded funny to him*. Don't spend time wondering why you can't laugh at the wit in the disparagement. Wonder, instead, about his maturity.

Any time you are put down, disparaged, denigrated, or ridiculed, or just don't like what you're hearing try responding emphatically with, "I'm wondering. Now that you have said that (put me down) (interrupted me) (laughed at me), do you feel more important? I'd like you to think about this."

Then disengage. Leave the room or tell him you are taking a time out. In any case, you will make a greater impact upon your mate if you take this approach. Don't carry on any discussion. You might say, "I don't want to talk about it" or "I'll get back to you later" if he continues to challenge you.

Responding to Blocking and Diverting

Stay aware and alert to your feelings. If you feel frustrated when you are asking your mate about something of concern to you or when you are trying to tell him about something which is important to you, you may be experiencing blocking and diverting.

Since you have a right to manage your affairs, if you are being blocked and diverted from gaining the information you need, then your boundaries are being violated. You are being thwarted in a sneaky, covert way, as if you did not have basic rights. This is an assault upon your human dignity.

143

If you are asking a question and are being blocked and diverted, do *not* respond to the statements that are being thrown at you like roadblocks and do *not* respond to the statements that are diverting you from your purpose. Say, "Look at me!" then keep repeating your question or statement.

For example,

> *"Where did the $5,000 go?"*
> *"Are you telling me I have to sort through all this when you don't even balance your checkbook?"*
> *"Look at me! Where did the $5,000 go?"*
> *"If you don't like my bookkeeping then you do the taxes from now on. I've had it with you."*
> *"Look at me! Where did the $5,000 go?"*

Repeat your question until he responds to it. Stay focused on your own feelings—your desire to know. Don't get caught by his words. It would be easy to want to defend yourself, but if you did you would then be diverted. His response might be either a direct answer to your question or a direct statement telling you he will not answer your question. Neither is blocking or diverting.

If you wish, you might say, "Stop diverting me!"

Responding to Accusation and Blame

Responding with awareness to accusation and blame is *crucial* if the partner is to live free from abuse. This is so because awareness of accusation and blame as well as the knowledge that accusation and blame are abusive frees the partner to leave the abuser if he does not stop the abuse.

Another way to express this is that a partner may stay in an abusive relationship because she believes that she can explain to her mate that she is not doing what she is accused of doing and that she is not responsible for what she is blamed for. The partner wants her mate to understand her and to realize that she is not his enemy.

If you experience verbal abuse in your relationship, then, without a doubt, you experience accusation and blame.

You can respond most effectively to accusation and blame when you recognize it and fully realize that verbal abusers blame and accuse the people they abuse. When you are accused and blamed you are abused.

When you are yelled at, snapped at, told that you are acting wrong, acting smart, acting dumb, trying to start a fight, imagining things, twisting things around, interrupting, trying to have the last word, going on and on, thinking wrong, thinking you're smart, thinking you know it all, picking a fight, asking for it, looking wrong, looking in the wrong way, looking for trouble, trying to start an argument, and so forth, you are being abused. Respond with, "Stop accusing and blaming me right now! Stop it!"

You might choose to add any of the following:

"Don't let me ever hear you say that again!"

"Remember whom you're talking to!"

"Don't talk to me like that!"

"I think you know better than that!"

Don't spend a second trying to explain that you weren't doing what you were accused of doing or guilty of what you were blamed for. Just say, "Stop it." Abusive statements are lies about you which are told to you. They violate your boundaries. The abuser in effect invades your mind, makes up a "story" about your motives, and then tells it to you. No human being has the right to do that to another.

Generally, accusing and blaming involve lies about the partner's intentions, attitudes, and motives. They leave her feeling frustrated and misunderstood and, therefore, especially desirous of explaining herself. If she does try to explain herself, the abuse is perpetuated.

One more word about "explaining." If you are encountering abuse and feel that if you could explain things he'd understand, remember this: If someone started throwing rocks through your windows, you would be more inclined to tell him to stop than you would be to explain to him why he shouldn't throw rocks. Verbal abuse is like a rock thrown through your window.

Responding to Judging and Criticizing

Usually judgments and criticism are lies about one's personal qualities and performance. They are blows to self-esteem. When you hear judgments and criticism such as "You're a lousy driver," it might be helpful to ask yourself, "Who presumes a right or authority to judge and criticize me? Who is the critic? Who is making the judgement?" Not a court of law, nor a supreme court justice, nor a god, but someone who should be minding his own business.

No one has the right to judge and criticize your personal qualities and performance. Defining you violates your boundaries.

145

The presumption is an invasion. To respond to judging and criticizing, speak as strongly, firmly, emphatically, and authoritatively as you can and let the energy of your anger support you:

"Do you hear yourself?"

"Stop judging me!"

"Cut out the criticism!"

"Enough of that."

"I don't accept that."

"That's nonsense!"

"Please keep your comments to yourself."

"Mind your own business, please!"

"This is not your concern!"

Then disengage, leave the area if at all possible, and certainly don't continue with a discussion. Further discussion dilutes the impact of your response.

Responding to Trivializing

Trivializing is abusive behavior which makes light of your work, your efforts, your interests, or your concerns. It is done very covertly, often with feigned innocence. The abuser invades your boundaries and moves into your psyche by telling you that what is meaningful to you has little meaning—what is valuable to you has little value. He attempts to dilute meaning and value in your life.

When you hear trivializing you might respond with any of the following:

"I certainly don't feel supported when I hear that kind of talk."

"I'd rather not be hearing this from you."

"I've heard all I want to hear from you."

Responding to Undermining

Because undermining is cruel and covert, the best response is to "tell it like it is:"

"I don't like your attitude!"

"That felt like a low blow."

"Cut that out!"

"I am definitely not having any fun with you."

One type of abuser will laugh if his mate accidentally hurts herself. If, for example, she falls in the mud or burns herself spilling the soup, the abuser expresses hilarity.

This type of abuse undermines the partner's self-esteem and is an expression of the abuser's sadistic tendencies. It invades the partner's boundaries violating her experience of reality. The abuser is saying, "That is not hurtful. That is something which gives pleasure. See me laugh."

Responding to Threatening

If you are physically threatened or threatened with physical harm (including sexual assault—married or not) or perceive a situation that seems as if it might become physically threatening, or if you feel that your or your family's well-being is threatened, it is extremely important that you find support and help as soon as possible.

If you are verbally threatened in other ways, your mate is trying to manipulate you. If you don't do what he wants, for example, he threatens to leave, stay out all night, say "no" to you the next time you ask him for something, and so forth. In this case, the threat of "pending disaster" shatters the partner's serenity as well as her boundaries.

Respond as clearly and as calmly as you possibly can with "Don't bother me with those threats, please," or "Stop threatening me!" or "I don't want to hear it!" or "Leave me alone!"

Responding to Name Calling

Name calling, as described earlier, is an invasion of your boundaries. Since name calling is outrageously abusive, it should be responded to with outrage.

"Stop that! Don't ever, ever, call me names!"

"I don't want to hear any name calling in this house/ around here/anymore!"

If you have been called names, it is very important that you realize that no one ever, for any reason, has a right to call you names. There is no justification for name calling. If you have become accustomed to being called names, it is also important to keep in mind that it is possible to live your life free from this kind of abuse: many people do. There is a strong possibility that a name-caller does not have, and may not gain, the requisite emotional development to love another in a healthy relationship.

Responding to Ordering

If your mate gives you orders, he has forgotten that you are a separate person with the right to life, liberty, and the pursuit of happiness, that you are a free person, and that if he wants something of you, he must make a courteous request. You might remind him of your boundaries and call this to his attention by saying "Who are you giving orders to?" or "Do you hear yourself?" or "Can you say please nicely?" or "I don't follow orders!"

If he gives you orders beginning with "we," as for example, "We're leaving right now," you might in this instance remind him of your boundaries by saying, "That's not what I had in mind."

Responding to Forgetting and Denial

You cannot respond appropriately to denial if you believe the abuser. *Do not believe the abuser's denial,* or you may be caught in the endless cycle of trying to explain to him how he hurts or frightens you and just how disturbing some of his behavior is.

If you become stuck in this cycle of needing to explain, it may be because you believe that there is some way to gain your mate's understanding. When he says that he doesn't know what you're talking about, you may believe that you can explain to him what you are talking about. However, this is not possible.

Responding with authority to angry or raging denial is an additional problem. Without really thinking about it, the madder he gets the harder the partner may try to explain herself so that he won't be so mad. The more she explains, the madder he gets, so the more she tries. Then the more he denies. This is the cycle of "trying to explain."

Since abusers claim that their partners "make" them mad, the partner often believes that she has somehow thrown her mate into a rage, and all because he has misunderstood her or she has said something wrong. She may *assume* that when she can get him to understand what she meant, he'll stop raging and at last be happier with her.

If the partner believes the abuser's denial, she might also become stuck in another way. She might become stuck trying to overcome or transcend her hurt, having decided that "no matter what" she shouldn't be disturbed because, after all, *he* says "she's taking it all wrong."

The trickiest form of denial is forgetting. Be aware that forgetting is a form of denial that shifts all responsibility from the abuser to some "weakness of mind." "I don't remember saying that" leaves the partner wishing she had a witness.

How can you tell him you are upset by something he said if he says that you made it up and that he didn't say it? The key here is: Don't tell him later you were upset "when . . ." Don't give him a chance to deny the abuse or to discount your feelings. Instead, when you hear something you don't like, respond *immediately* with words that tell him in no uncertain terms to "Cut it out."

The two most effective responses to denial are "Stop it" and "Stop making me crazy!"

In order not to be confused by denial, keep your attention focused upon your own feelings and bodily sensations. Don't for a minute try to figure out what your mate is thinking or feeling. Don't for a second think about whether he'll understand why you're telling him to stop it. Don't for even a split second wonder whether he'll like your response.

If you feel the hurt, pain, or confusion of abuse, don't spend time trying to understand your mate or how he could be saying what he's saying. If you don't like it, respond in a way that lets him know you want him to stop *right now.*

If he does tell you he doesn't remember an incident that was disturbing to you, don't accept his "forgetting" denial. Simply say, "I don't believe you. And I don't want it to happen again."

Responding to Abusive Anger

While reading the responses throughout this section, if you noticed yourself thinking or feeling that you would be afraid to respond as suggested, you may be in a relationship with an anger addict. If so, you must respect your fear and yourself and follow the caution near the beginning of this chapter.

Abusive anger is a very significant factor in verbal abuse and seems to be closely linked to the need to "blow up," to dominate, to control, to go one up, and to put down.

How do you respond to abusive anger? The women I spoke with who had encountered abusive anger all felt afraid of this kind of anger, and not without reason.

A general rule for dealing with an angry man is to stay away from him. However, if you are being snapped at and yelled at, you may need to have some strategies of response which make an impact on your mate, which motivate change in your mate or which give you time to get out of the relationship if necessary.

If your mate yells and snaps at you, you may feel too stunned to respond. You may, however, be able to distance yourself somewhat from him by thinking of him not as your husband, or the father of your children, or a friend, or your champion, or kin, but, instead, as a petulant, screaming, tantrum-throwing, recalcitrant, or argumentative child. If you can bring one of these images to mind the next time he yells at you, you might respond with, "You may *not* raise your voice to me" or "I don't like that tone of voice." Or you might be quick enough to say, "Stop! Take a deep breath and please talk nicely."

An angry man may abuse you around friends in a way which has meaning only to you. In this situation, if you speak up, you may appear to be "out of line" or "making something up." Try responding with, "Although no one here knows what this is about, I am *very* displeased with you."

Many partners find responding to abusive anger particularly difficult. This anger not only is unexpected but is usually expressed with words which catch the partner by surprise. "What is he thinking? What does he mean?" Her mind is searching, analyzing, trying to understand what he's yelling about and what it means in relation to her.

The key to responding to abusive anger is *don't pay any attention to the words*. When you are being snapped at or yelled at you are being abused. Consequently, you do not need to spend a second taking it in, analyzing it, or trying to understand it.

If you, like most partners, find it exceedingly difficult to respond to abusive anger, try to stay alert in the present for the signs of anger. The moment you hear anger in the tone of his voice, respond with "Hold it!" then leave or, if you are talking to him on the phone, hang up. The moment you see the rigid, tense, ready-to-explode appearance of his face and body, respond with, "Hold it!" or leave. The moment you sense his tension in any way, leave.

These responses may help you to make an impact and avoid abuse. If you can become aware of the anger attack the moment it starts so that you can stop it or get away immediately you may break the pattern of being caught by the abuser's words. If you don't get hooked into trying to understand the words, you can respond more quickly and with greater clarity.

You cannot change anyone. If your mate is abusive and does not choose to change, you may have to confront the reality that you cannot live a healthy life in an unhealthy environment. You were not meant to live your life being on guard, ever prepared to respond to abuse. Furthermore, the absence of abuse does not necessarily guarantee a warm, caring, happy relationship.

If possible, solve the problem before it starts. The best way to avoid verbal abuse in a relationship is to spot any potential abuser and avoid a relationship with him in the first place.

If you are considering a new relationship, be discriminating. Notice the difference between what you want, what you imagine, and what you are actually getting. Notice if you and your new mate share the same reality.

The following questions serve as a means of evaluation. You must trust your own perceptions and feelings to answer these questions. If you come up with even one answer you don't like, there is a good chance you will not have a healthy relationship.

Does he have a sense of joy in life?

Do you enjoy his ideas, and do you feel a rapport with him?

Do you feel a real connection, laughing together and catching meanings in the same way?

Is there a best-friend quality to your relationship?

Do you feel relaxed with him?

Can you really be yourself without criticism?

Does he share his interests with you and express an interest in yours?

Does he speak openly and honestly about himself?

Do you feel warmth and understanding from him?

Is his humor often at the expense of others, or is it bitter or intimidating, or does it make you uncomfortable?

Does he seem distrustful of a number of other people?

Does he argue against your thoughts, ideas, feelings, and experiences?

Is time spent with him not as pleasant as you usually anticipate?

Is his world composed of "good guys" and "bad guys"?

Does he seem to understand or remember things differently from you?

Does he make assumptions about you based on anecdotal evidence?

Whether you are, were, or never have been in an abusive relationship, the questions above present some criteria by which you might evaluate any old or new relationship. Most important of all are your own feelings. If you experience the slightest feeling that something is wrong, *it is.*

CHAPTER XIII

Recovery

All changes, even the most longed for, have their
melancholy; for what we leave behind us is a part
of ourselves; we must die to one life before we can
enter into another!

— *Anatole France*

When the partners of verbal abusers recognize the abuse and take
the necessary steps to ensure that they are no longer subject to it,
they are already in the process of recovery. Recovery is a process of
healing and reorientation that does not follow a fixed schedule
and takes different amounts of time for different people.

The recognition of abuse, whether it be emotional, physical,
or sexual, whether it occurred in childhood or in adulthood,
brings both pain and shock. The spirit is wrenched from its foun-
dations as mind and body confront the inconceivable, which must
in the end be recognized as a reality, realized, and integrated. The
longer the abuse has been perpetuated and the more intense it has
been, the longer the process of recovery may take.

In her book *Stopping Wife Abuse*, Jennifer Baker Fleming lists
affirmations which support women in thinking of themselves in
stronger and more positive ways (1979, p. 64). I include the list here
with changes and additions to support victims of verbal abuse.

I can trust my own feelings and perceptions.

I am not to blame for being verbally abused.

I am not the cause of another's irritation, anger, or rage.

I deserve freedom from mental anguish.

I can say no to what I do not like or want.

I do not have to take it.

I am an important human being.

I am a worthwhile person.

I deserve to be treated with respect.

I have power over my own life.

I can use my power to take good care of myself.

I can decide for myself what is best for me.

I can make changes in my life if I want to.

I am not alone; I can ask others to help me.

I am worth working for and changing for.

I deserve to make my own life safe and happy.

I can count on my creativity and resourcefulness.

Following are some guidelines for recovery and healing from abuse. They may be helpful to you if you have been in a verbally abusive relationship or are in the process of leaving one. As you free yourself from the abusive environment, you can take steps to enhance your self-esteem and to improve the quality of your life.

Recovery from verbal abuse is the opportunity to accept all your feelings and to recognize their validity. You may be the first person to recognize and accept them and to know that they are not wrong. They are, as we have said earlier, indicators that something is or was wrong in your environment, *and it isn't you.*

If you do not have a supportive professional counselor or therapist, it is worth your time and money to look for one. A counselor can give you needed support in creating a nourishing environment for yourself. With the support of a counselor, you may also become aware of instances in childhood where you adapted to verbal abuse or saw others adapt to it. At home, in school, or with peers, you may have been led to doubt your own feelings. Even the most well-meaning parents cannot always understand and accept the feelings of their children.

Be sure that you feel nurtured and supported by your counselor. Advice on how to improve the relationship can actually be counterproductive. Just as the physically battered wife feels responsible for being hit, so, too, the verbally battered wife feels she is responsible for being yelled at or put down.

Beware of well-meaning but unaware counseling. One partner was told "If you open up to him, he'll open up to you." In general, this is not true of the verbal abuser. He will be aware of your vulnerability, and when he's feeling angry he may use it against you. Some abusers feel triumphant, as if they have won, if their mates feel hurt. Some fly into a rage, claiming that they are being attacked, if their partner tells them when she feels hurt.

One partner, separated and planning to divorce an abuser, heard from her counselor, "You'll always be in a relationship with him through the children." She said, "I thought and felt, 'I'll never get away. I'll always be a target, as if I were standing in front of a machine gun.'" She came to realize that this is not true. She never has to be in the same room with him and she never has to talk to him.

Another counselor who had no experience with verbal abuse said to a verbally abused woman, "He's just a pussycat. Look how he provides for you, and he doesn't run around." If she had seen physical evidence of the abuse, she would never have said this, even facetiously. Verbal abuse doesn't leave physical evidence.

See the annotated bibliography at the end of this book for books that address recovery issues. These books may provide insights and encouragement. Although they are not explicitly directed toward the issue of verbal abuse, they may provide additional support.

Look for a support group you feel comfortable with. It can be a great aid to recovery from the effects of verbal abuse. A support group is especially valuable to those who have suffered from verbal abuse that was then denied by the abuser. Being with others who understand and have had the same experience nourishes the spirit. A support group which can give you honest feedback and a sense of community and can validate your feelings and experience is most desirable.

Taking step-by-step action toward personal goals and meaningful work builds confidence and self-esteem. No matter how you feel, you can usually act in a way that is nourishing to yourself, setting a goal, no matter how small, and completing it daily.

While you are going through internal and external changes, keep structure and constants in your daily life. Keep regular hours for eating, exercising, and sleeping.

Recognize that all change, even the most longed-for change, is stressful. When you are going through change, do everything possible to nurture and care for yourself.

Focus on living in the present, and use all of the energy available to you to love and care for yourself.

Protect yourself, and meet your needs with a fatherly and motherly attitude toward yourself. This attitude is both nourishing and confident. A fatherly attitude includes the spirit of exploration and adventure and the courage to act. A motherly attitude includes the spirit of loving acceptance of yourself, your feelings, your ideas, your creativity, and the child within you.

On the path of recovery, you may encounter the realization that you have been a victim. Women who have been dominated and controlled by their mates either overtly or covertly are part of a tradition thousands of years old. It may grieve you, but if you feel ashamed, it is the abuser's shame that you have taken in. By recognizing his reality as separate from yours, you can more readily see where the shame belongs. Your recognition of the abuse and the steps you have taken to free yourself from it initiate you into a new tradition of Reality II self-esteem and freedom from abuse.

You may wonder how you could have become confused by verbal abuse. Double messages, such as when the abuser says, "I'm not mad! I don't know what you're talking about!" while he sounds mad and does know what he's talking about, are always confusing. Now, by giving your feelings and perceptions priority, double messages will not betray you. For example, if you hear his anger even when he says he's not angry, your perception of his anger takes priority over his words. You *know* he is angry because you hear his anger.

On this path of recovery you may encounter new realizations of what you suffered from the abuse. If you had experienced abuse that shocked you and left you feeling confused and off balance, you may now experience flashbacks. These occur because the initial experience was traumatizing. It was more than you could understand and integrate at the time. A flashback is like a sudden recognition and re-experiencing of the pain and reality of a shocking past experience. Recognizing what is happening, working through the feelings that come with the flashback, and staying focused and involved in the present are all helpful.

You may also need time to sort through the confusing messages you were given about yourself. If you were repeatedly told that you do not know what you are talking about, or if all your views and perceptions were countered, you will need time to experience the correspondence between your perceptions and the reality around you without interference.

When you have gone quite a way down the path of recovery, you may begin a possible new relationship. Now that you have recognized verbal abuse and learned to discriminate between your reality and the abuser's, you can trust yourself to perceive the slightest hint of a Reality I personality. If all is not well, it will only get worse.

As you travel this path, you are likely to discover new talents, new abilities, and new perceptions of yourself. If your best abilities were continuously discounted or trivialized, you may find that what you thought were your failings are instead your gifts. The spirit thrives when it is free and nourished.

As you more fully recognize the abuse that you suffered, you may encounter feelings that you never expected. If you are giving up the illusion of a relationship and the loss of a dream, you may find that you will grieve the loss of all that you did not have—all that you missed.

Part of the process of recovery is the grieving of loss, and part of the grieving of loss is the recovery of the spirit. In life, much of what one grieves one never had. For example, the partner may realize she was never accepted by her mate because of his overwhelming need to control and dominate her. Her grief would be an acknowledgment that a human need was not met—a value not attained. She could not feel this kind of loss—the loss of what she never had—unless her spirit knew its needs and rights.

In this sense, grief is the conscious acknowledgment and realization of what the spirit already knows. Through grief we *consciously* become aware of a value of the spirit and by grieving the loss, we recover in such a way that we integrate that value. Thus we become more whole.

When the victim of verbal abuse realizes that she was not loved, only controlled, she grieves the lack of love because she knows that she is lovable. Through that process she gains Reality II self-esteem. She knows that she is worthy of love and respect.

CHAPTER XIV

Looking Back

Now it seems like everything is real. Before, it was like I was in the wrong world. My being here was a big mistake. I made him so mad.

— *A Partner*

The first thing I noticed about Olivia was her eyes, large and dark; they laughed like crystal glittering. She had promised me an interview and now, after several delays, we were in a little restaurant, drinking coffee, past the pleasantries, reaching for the marrow of our purpose.

"I wasn't always this happy," she said. "I'll never forget the day my husband turned into a stranger right in front of me." She hesitated. "But most of the time I don't think about it."

"You do look happy," I said.

"Oh, yes, in spite of everything, life is sweet. I haven't been put down or yelled at in a very long time. If I do meet that kind of person, I'm gone. Like it doesn't take two minutes to spot it.

"It used to be almost every day I felt hurt and was trying to understand it."

Her perplexing past flashed across her face.

"And your life started changing when you had this stranger experience?" I asked. "Can you tell me about it?"

She shrugged and looked around, as if to make sure no one was listening. We had the café to ourselves.

"All by myself. All by myself," she repeated.

I nodded encouragingly, wondering, "Had she found her husband with another woman, or what?"

"All by myself, I realized that Dick (my ex) was really in a different world. We'd been married for sixteen years when I suddenly knew—I really knew that what he'd been doing all that time had been wrong. Do you know what I mean?"

I nodded. "Yes," I said, noticing that her thin, fragile look belied the strength in her voice.

"For a long time I hadn't known it. It was strange—if it had been happening to someone else I could have said, 'Hey, that's wrong!' but it was years, sixteen I guess [she smiled] before I really knew it for me."

"Do you mean it didn't seem that he was doing something really wrong when he yelled at you and put you down?" I asked.

"Well, yes, that's it. I'd known for a long time I wasn't happy with the way things were, but somehow I thought I should have been able to stand it, as if I were wrong to feel hurt, or maybe I should just feel differently about it. Why did I have to feel that bad when he said it was 'nothing'? I thought I should be able to get him to understand me so he wouldn't get so mad at me."

More coffee was poured. "It sounds as if you're saying you used to think it was wrong to feel hurt when he yelled at you. How come? What do you think it was that made you feel that way?" I asked.

She closed her eyes, tilting her head up as if to capture an old scene. Her head came down, she looked straight at me, eyes wide: "He always had a reason [for being mad] that seemed to make sense to him. That's why. But after the day he turned into a stranger I stopped thinking I was wrong."

I turned the tape over in the recorder. She waited.

"Can you tell me," I asked, "all about what happened and how you felt about it? I'd like to know—to understand this kind of thing."

"Yeah, here's what happened. It wasn't, I guess, so much what happened that changed my life, as it was that *finally understanding it* changed my life."

She began: "We had friends staying at the house. They'd stayed over. The evening before, before Dick got home, they'd talked about how she was going to fix soft-boiled eggs and toast for them both and did I have eggs and bread? I said, 'yes, plenty,' and asked if they wanted anything else? 'No.' For sure that was all they wanted. That was their favorite.

"In the morning, when I was in the garden having my coffee and they were getting up, Dick came around the corner of the house, suddenly appearing right in front of me, saying, 'I'm going to the store for some coffee cake.' (as he did almost every Sunday) and, 'Do you need anything?' I was kind of relaxed and pleased he asked because it seemed thoughtful. I thought a moment of what I might need and what I had in the kitchen and how much coffee cake was needed to go around and the eggs and toast they were having. I thought this all at once (you know how you do) and I knew that I didn't need anything. I mean I didn't keep him waiting or anything.

"I said 'Thanks, I don't think I need anything. They probably won't be having any coffee cake.'

"Right then Dick became furious. His face went red. His eyes glared. His jaws clenched. He lurched at me. I was scared he was so loud. His words were like bullets the way they seemed to hit me. 'I don't care! I'm not buying it for them! I'm buying it for me!' And he was gone. He'd stepped back around the corner, disappearing as suddenly as he'd appeared."

Olivia had been off in her own world, staring into space while she talked. She glanced toward me, raising her eyebrows slightly as if remembering the strangeness of it.

"It seems kind of impossible now, that he could get as mad as that, but it did happen. It seems, now that I look back, like something he could do very easily.

"Right then I didn't feel anything. I guess what they call shock is what happened. If it was shock, it was familiar shock. I went kind of numb, and the birds stopped singing or I didn't hear them. I don't know. And later I felt all stirred up inside somewhere between my heart and my stomach.

"As I look back, I remember that I was trying to make some sense out of it—what I'd said, what he'd said."

She hesitated, took a deep breath. I caught her eye, "At that time, when you were trying to make sense of it, were you also feeling 'all stirred up' inside?"

Nodding gently, as if she was rocking herself, she said, "Yeah, maybe feeling that way made it hard to think. Finally, when I did get it figured out, that's when my life changed. But now I'm getting ahead of myself.

"Now, I know that whether you get hit with a fist or hit with words, it's not right, but then, I was trying to make sense of it.

"So I started trying to figure out what I'd said to hurt him so bad that he'd yell at me so. I didn't know then that I was the only one hurting. I was thinking, 'Was he mad that I knew why they weren't having coffee cake and he didn't?'"

"So you thought he might feel left out and have had hurt feelings over it?" I asked.

"Yes, I thought maybe I should have known better than to let him know I knew their plans.

"I thought, 'If only I'd told him why, but could I remember to give reasons in similar cases? How was I to know? Or, was he mad that I assumed he'd buy enough to share and he didn't want to share?'"

"So you thought another reason he might be mad was that you presumed he'd share his coffee cake without asking him first if he'd mind?" I asked.

"Yes, I thought, 'If only I'd not assumed.' But did I assume? Or, was he mad because he wanted to share the coffee cake and disappointed that he probably couldn't?"

I found myself concentrating on the many possibilities she'd explored while trying to understand. "So you thought maybe if he wasn't mad at your assumption, then maybe he was mad that he couldn't share the coffee cake?"

"Yes, that's what I was trying to figure out. Did I disappoint him? But I didn't mean to. Was he mad because he'd planned to buy two coffee cakes and now he had to change his thinking? All because of me."

"So you thought his having to change plans made him mad?"

Olivia nodded, "I thought, maybe he was planning to get extra cake to make a party atmosphere and he was so disappointed he was furious and was just saying he didn't care and was buying just for himself so I wouldn't know how disappointed he was. Or maybe he was yelling at me because he thought I knew he was disappointed and I didn't show I cared.

"Or, was he mad that I was out there enjoying the yard and not going to the store for him?

"How was I to know?"

I shook my head, "I don't know. I don't know how you could have known. I guess you must have felt that if you understood, got it right, you'd never make the same mistake, whatever it was, and then you'd never have to go through another one of those shattering experiences. Would you say so?"

"Oh, yeah, I've no doubt about that. I think that, by then, trying to understand was overriding everything else in my life. Do you know what I mean?"

"I do," I said. Then I asked, "Aren't you saying that you focused more and more and more on trying to understand?"

Olivia's eyes sparkled as she leaned forward: "That's it."

She continued, "I was wrong about every reason—I mean about why he went into a rage. Later I got up enough courage to ask him what he'd been mad about. (I steeled myself for what might happen—no more getting caught off guard.) He said, 'What do you mean mad?' and all that, as he usually did. I felt strange. I didn't say anything. I kept waiting. Then he said that I hadn't wanted him to buy any coffee cake! That's what he said. And I can hear him all angry again when he said that. I was really confused that he'd think that, with him making lots of money and buying coffee cake nearly every Sunday.

"That evening I thought about how hopeful I'd always been. One time I had what I thought was a really good idea. I asked him to ask me what I meant before he got mad. I thought that would really solve a lot of problems since I was sure he wanted to understand me more than anything. He said I was making a big deal out of nothing.

"At the time I hadn't given up the hope that even if I *was* 'making a big deal out of nothing,' he'd understand and that if he just did this little thing, it would be so much better for both of us. He'd find out I hadn't meant anything to upset him, and I'd be able to explain before he got so disturbed.

"But, somehow, in some way, I wasn't able to get across to him that these incidents which he said I had blown all out of proportion felt even bigger to me than I was able to say."

"I see. Now, I'm wondering if your beginning realization that he wasn't the way you'd always thought he was contributed to your feeling of being 'all stirred up inside.'"

"Yes," Olivia responded quickly, "I'm sure of it now. I can see that it was so confusing because nothing fit. I couldn't get a handle on what was happening all those years. The strange stuff was always there. It didn't seem to fit together with my image of him, which was of a mature man, husband, father, and respected professional."

"So he never did ask you what you meant before he got mad at you."

"Right. He never did."

"Eventually, I got him to go to a counselor with me. He said that he was really trying and I wasn't. So I tried even harder. Looking back I can see that I was confused and didn't know it. He said he loved me—and wasn't love all those things you hear about being kind and considerate. He must be thinking about it every day—if he loved me, but it didn't seem like it."

"I can see why it didn't seem like it. It was confusing, but you figured it out?"

"Yes. That Sunday, it kind of hit me, nobody should be yelling at me. If I can't figure out why I'm being yelled at, after trying for a whole day, then I shouldn't be yelled at. And who was it that was yelling at me? Well, it sure wasn't the man who loved me. That man wouldn't do that kind of thing. He had disappeared a long time ago, when I wasn't looking, and now I was looking at a stranger. And all that time I'd been thinking he was the man I'd married."

"What an experience—to have your husband turn into a stranger."

Olivia smiled, "Yeah, my whole life started changing right there. Looking back, I can see that even if I'd said, 'I don't want you to buy coffee cake this Sunday' (as I never would have done or even imagined), there would have been no way he could make it right to attack me like he did. It was wrong, and it wasn't me that was wrong. That's what I'm getting at. Now I feel that inside."

"So," I said, "no matter what he was thinking, he had no right."

"Right!" she laughed. "Now I know the way it should have been. If my husband hadn't turned into a stranger, it would have been that if I'd said, 'I don't want you to buy the coffee cake,' he'd have said, 'Oh! Why not?'—kind of surprised."

She paused, her eyes asking if I knew what she meant. I picked up her story, "And then you would have discussed it?"

"For sure," she said with certainty. "He'd have been interested to know why."

"That would have been what one would normally expect," I agreed. "Tell me, did he say he was sorry?"

"No, I can't say that he ever apologized, not for the abuse, not once in the sixteen years we were together.

"Looking back, I can see that he'd convinced me I made him mad. With that going on in my head I was never sure who should apologize!"

"And then?" I prompted.

"After I figured out what he was doing, I stopped trying to understand and trying to explain." She rolled her eyes, "I started trying to get him to stop. That was very hard, because he'd get angrier, or laugh, when I told him to cut it out.

"It was really hard too, because I always had a lot of feeling. You know, when I was little I used to pray to God that I'd grow up fast so I wouldn't feel anymore—like the grownups around me." Her eyes glistened. "He never gave any signs of feeling, that's for sure."

"But you kept on feeling?"

"Yeah—especially feeling sad. Looking back, I can say that in the end it was my feelings that saved me." Her eyes grew large. "All that pain was there because my soul knew it wasn't right before I knew it. My feelings were right all along. It's wrong to be where you're put down and yelled at, no matter how much the other person says he's not putting you down and not yelling. Don't they usually yell that they're not yelling?"

"Yes," I agreed, "they do."

"One last thing I want to tell you is that, as I looked back at the whole relationship, I realized that he put down what I did best because that's what he was jealous of. Anyway, I had ended up not knowing what I did best, and so it turns out that what I did worst was what I thought I did best and what I did best was what I thought I did worst. So after a while I didn't think I could do anything."

"Well," I assured her, "you're not alone. That happens to people who are dominated and controlled. It's a sign of abuse."

She smiled, "I've got it pretty much sorted out now. I've been so much happier."

"I'm glad. You've shared so much. Thank you."

"Well, I'm glad, too, that I had a chance to get this off my chest. Isn't that where the pain is, in the heart?"

*   *   *

As the former partners of verbal abusers looked back at their experiences, these are some of the statements they made.

"Before, I thought: if he loves me, how can he be hostile? Now I think: if he's hostile how can he love me?"

"Before, I thought he just couldn't talk. Now I know that he was staying aloof."

"Before, I believed he was trying to understand me as much as I was trying to understand him. Now I know that that wasn't on his mind."

"Before, I couldn't understand how he could put me down and then say he hadn't said what he said. I thought he had a split personality. Now I know that he didn't."

"Before, I thought that what I thought was wrong. Now I know that was because he said everything was the opposite of what I thought."

"Before, I thought he was kind of handicapped about talking. I brought up all kinds of subjects, but he wouldn't talk to me. I tried to be entertaining. Now I can see that he was trying to stay distant and in control."

"Before, I had this strange fear that if I expressed a personal view it would be wrong. He just couldn't accept my view. By the time he was through I'd feel confused and defeated. Now I know that what he was doing was countering me."

"Before, I thought he didn't know how much things he said upset me, and as soon as he knew he'd apologize. Now I know that he didn't apologize because he thought that would be giving in."

"Before, I believed him when he said 'I love you,' so I couldn't see his opposition for what it was."

"Before, I thought that if I worked hard enough at it, I would be able to understand why he got angry. Now I know that he was irrational, so I couldn't understand."

"Before, I thought that all men think differently from women, but for some reason I was one of the only women in the world who hadn't figured out how to talk to a man so he wouldn't get mad."

"Before, I thought that, since we were married, he must be on my side like family and that he had my best interests at heart; now I realize that he thought he had a right to control me just because we were married."

"Before, I thought he wouldn't say things if they weren't true; now I know he doesn't think like that."

"Now that it's over I realize that I liked to be near trees and plants because I felt safe with them. They didn't hurt me."

CHAPTER XV

The Underlying Dynamics: Some Reasons Why

> . . . he had never thought of her (ah how it hugely glared at him!) but in the chill of his egotism and the light of her use . . . . This horror of waking— *this* was knowledge, knowledge under the breath of which the very tears of his eyes seemed to freeze.
>
> — *Henry James*, The Beast in the Jungle

Although no two verbally abusive relationships are exactly alike, they do seem to share certain underlying dynamics. The following exploration of these dynamics draws upon Alice Miller's research into the effects of early childhood experiences on adult behavior and Karen Horney's development of the concept of the ideal image.

If we assume that both the abuser and the partner grew up in Reality I, we are confronted with a number of questions. For example, why has the partner become a victim? Why has the abuser become a persecutor? Why has the partner emerged into Reality II without Reality II self-esteem? And why has the abuser remained in Reality I seeking Power Over and dominance instead of mutuality?

I believe that an understanding of the early childhood experiences of both the partner and the abuser may begin to answer these questions. Let us begin this exploration with the partner's childhood.

CHILDHOOD EXPERIENCES OF THE PARTNER

In childhood the typical partner lived in Reality I where the power adults have over children was misused, often through ignorance, and often with the best of intentions. Here, dominance and Power Over prevailed and hence so did verbal abuse. In this reality, many of the partner's feelings could neither be validated nor accepted. In some cases, she had an indifferent, absent, uninvolved, or angry father. In some cases primary caretakers, relatives, or teachers were verbally abusive.

In spite of all this, there seems to have been one decisive circumstance which allowed the partner to emerge into Reality II. This was that in childhood she *did* have some sympathetic witness to her experience—some thread still connected her to the knowledge that she suffered and that something was wrong. But what? To her, the all-powerful adults were not wrong. How could they be? They were godlike to her infant eyes. Her only alternative was to believe that something must be wrong with the way she was—how she expressed herself, how she came across, or possibly with her feelings and experience of reality itself.

Consequently, the partner emerged into Reality II without Reality II self-esteem. She knew that she suffered. She could, therefore, feel empathy and compassion for others. She did seek mutuality and understanding. The one thing she did not know was why she suffered.

Surely, the one who said he loved her would not be so upset with her, would not yell at her, nor tell her what was wrong with her, unless there was something wrong with the way she was, or how she came across. She easily believed that she might have said or done something inadvertently, or unconsciously, that hurt her mate just as she was hurting. She searched her soul for answers and surely, she thought, he did also. The last thing she would ever have imagined was that he could not search for answers because he could not share her reality.

We know that verbal abuse occurs to some extent in all but the most ideal of childhoods, leaving most with some uncertainty—some self-doubt. This self-doubt is greatly increased in an abusive relationship. For example, when the partner hears, "You're just trying to be right" or "You're taking it all wrong," what she had heard in childhood is reiterated in adulthood, but this time without a sympathetic witness; this time, behind closed doors.

Clearly, when there is no witness to one's experience and no validation of one's reality, one must rely solely upon one's own feelings and judgment. This is difficult for anyone. It is doubly difficult for the partner because the abuse itself diminishes her ability to trust her own feelings and her own judgment. Her feelings and judgment are constantly condemned by the abuse.

The victim of abuse is taught to believe that although she is hurting, she shouldn't be, or that she is in some way responsible. From childhood, she is conditioned not to understand her feelings and so not to recognize the truth. This truth is that she is being abused and blamed for the abuse (as if it could be justified) and for feeling bad about it (as if her feelings were wrong).

The typical partner believed the abuser's denial and so became frustrated and confused even while she searched for answers. Unable to reach clarity and understanding, the partner was left with feelings of inadequacy and confusion. If her mate was not wrong, if he was not lying, if she did take things wrong, then she could believe only that "something must be wrong with the way she was—how she expressed herself, how she came across, or possibly with her feelings and experience of reality itself." Thus the doubts of childhood rose up once more. She kept her mind open to what she might hear that would reveal what was wrong—why she suffered. She became, therefore, the perfect victim.

The partner suffered many wrongs to her spirit. And, she did not know the meaning of her pain. However, because she remained aware of her feelings, she was connected to the spirit of life at her center—the source of her Personal Power. Eventually, it was the power of her feelings and the knowledge of her spirit which enabled her to recognize the abuse and, in so doing, gain Reality II self-esteem.

CHILDHOOD EXPERIENCES OF THE ABUSER

Now, let us look at the origins of the abuser's behavior. The typical abuser also grew up in Reality I, where Power Over and dominance prevailed, and hence so did verbal abuse. Also, as was the case with the partner, many of his feelings were neither validated nor accepted. However, unlike the partner, he had *no* compassionate witness to his experience. Without a compassionate witness, he could conclude only that *nothing was wrong*. If nothing was wrong at all, then all his painful feelings must not exist. Automatically he stopped feeling his painful feelings. He closed them off from awareness as one would close a door. And he did not know what he suffered.

In this way he closed the door on a part of himself. He became inured to Reality I. And, just as Hitler modeled his behavior after that of his brutal father, so, too, the abuser modeled his behavior after his childhood abusers. He became adept at verbal abuse.

Without the knowledge of his feelings—of what he suffered—he could not experience empathy and compassion and so could not cross the threshold into Reality II. This reality was now behind closed doors.

> *The absence or presence of a helping witness in childhood determines whether a mistreated child will become a despot who turns his repressed feelings of helplessness against others or an artist who can tell about his or her suffering. (Alice Miller,* The Untouched Key, *1990, p. 60)*

Since the abuser feels justified in his behavior and seems to have no comprehension of its effects, we can assume only that he is acting out his repressed feelings and is, therefore, acting compulsively. Abusers seek Power Over because they feel helpless. The helpless, painful feelings of childhood that "must not exist" and "must not be felt" do exist and, if not felt, are acted out.

A long time ago in the abuser's childhood, he closed the door on these feelings. To survive in childhood he could do no less. His feeling self, nonetheless, lived on behind closed doors. This feeling child within was, psychologically speaking, locked away in a tomb of agony.

The longer the child within is unrecognized, the more enraged it becomes, and consequently, the more rage the abuser acts out. Alice Miller tells us

> *As long as this child within is not allowed to become aware of what happened to him or her, a part of his or her emotional life will remain frozen, and sensitivity to the humiliations of childhood will therefore be dulled.*
>
> *All appeals to love, solidarity, and compassion will be useless if this crucial prerequisite of sympathy and understanding is missing. (Alice Miller,* For Your Own Good, *1983, p. xv)*

Typically, even though the partner tries to explain to her mate what bothers her, the abuse continues. Appeals to the abuser's compassion are fruitless, because the abuser is not empathetic. As Alice Miller points out, a sympathetic and understanding witness to a child's suffering is a crucial prerequisite to empathy in adult-

hood. Without empathy, the abuser cannot be sensitive to his partner's anguish.

He acts out his repressed feelings—doing to another what
was done to him in his childhood. Since he cannot feel his feelings,
he *must* act them out. This is what compels him to perpetuate the
abuse. Even so, his feelings of pain and powerlessness, harbored
since childhood, are never dispelled. They only increase and so,
also, does his abusive behavior.

Each specific instance of abuse does, however, momentarily
alleviate the abuser's hidden feelings of pain and powerlessness,
leaving in their stead a sense of Power Over. His need to keep the
overwhelming pain that "must not exist" at bay is an underlying
dynamic force which compels him to seek Power Over, control,
dominance, and superiority.

In addition to feelings of powerlessness, many abusers have a
deeply buried feeling of guilt for having separated from their
mothers. It is generally recognized that the infant, male or female,
first identifies with the mother. It is the male only, however, who
must completely break from this identification to become other
than female. The severing of this bond may result in feelings of
guilt, especially if the mother-son relationship is not psychologically sound.

If these feelings are unresolved, the male may deem himself
superior to that which he rejects and may hold in contempt all that
is ascribed to the feminine. In this way he may attempt to "justify"
his separation from his mother and so assuage his guilt.

In general, we may assume that the abuser has closed off and
denied a complex and diverse assemblage of feelings. If his feelings are denied, he himself is denied. Who then is the abuser? To
others, he is "hard to get to really know." To himself, he is who he
"thinks" he is—an *ideal image* he takes himself to be. (Karen Horney, 1992, pp. 96–114)

The abuser's sense of self is not grounded in the feelings of
his being but is, instead, a fragile construction of mind devoid of
Personal Power. Personal Power is felt as the ability to know, to
choose, and to create from the ground of one's being, that is, from
the awareness of one's true feelings. Without Personal Power, the
abuser constantly seeks to feel Power Over. He feels dominant, of
higher status or superior to his partner when he is abusive. Some
abusers even seem to crave the euphoria of Power Over.

Not only does the abuser hide his feelings from himself, but
he also hides his abusive behavior from himself. His ideal image

denies the reality of his motivations, his compulsions, and his actions. For example, an extremely tense, angry, and explosive abuser may describe himself as easygoing and relaxed. A critical, judging abuser may describe himself as accepting of everyone— taking people as they come. An undermining and trivializing or coldly indifferent abuser may describe himself as supportive of everything his partner does. And a countering, discounting abuser may describe himself as very open to differing views. Many verbal abusers describe themselves in the positive light of *all* of the above while they indulge in all categories of abuse.

The confirmed abuser can define himself and the interpersonal reality so convincingly that the partner may accept his definitions. Such acceptance and trust increase her confusion.

Many partners have reported that their mates' images or "Power-Over personae" shifted over time and in different circumstances. One partner said of her mate, "Sometimes he's Mr. Sullen. Sometimes he's Mr. Joviality. Sometimes he's Mr. Pontificating. Sometimes he's Mr. Automaton. Sometimes he's Mr. Savoir-faire. Sometimes he's Mr. Raging. But *to most people, he's Mr. Nice Guy.*"

The abuser's loss of his feeling self and consequent feelings of powerlessness usually compel him to increasing self-aggrandizement and a correspondingly greater disparagement of his partner. However, he cannot, by abuse, bring his stifled feeling self to life. Since he mistakes excitement for aliveness and triumph for strength, he remains in constant need of bolstering his ideal image.

Usually, verbal abusers who become physically abusive do not see themselves as abusive, even when they are arrested. The abuser's denial arises out of the conflict between who he thinks he is and his compulsion to act abusively. This denial is a defense against the shattering of his ideal image and an impending identity crisis. His very identity would be at stake if he were to admit to what he was doing. This is why verbal abusers do not sincerely apologize.

> *A strong person can acknowledge weakness; a confident person can acknowledge mistakes. One who really feels weak and inferior inside cannot do so . . . . Since abusive men secretly feel very weak, they work even harder at denying their feelings, projecting them onto available others, the most available being their wives. (Fleming, 1979, p. 287)*

The confirmed abuser identifies with (believes he is) his ideal image. Consequently, he cloaks his behavior in self-righteous denial. We might compare the abuser to the Wizard of Oz. Uncloaked he is no longer a horrendous force of Power Over others, but an unsure frightened person. This does not mean, however, that the partner can "help" him. Hitler, too, was an abused child acting out his repressed feelings as an adult as Alice Miller's book, *For Your Own Good*, so clearly demonstrates.

The abuser often supports his ideal image by gaining agreement from others. He will let slip, in the natural course of conversation, how supportive and appreciative he is of his partner. It is no wonder that many verbally battered women have been told how lucky they are to have such a wonderful mate.

Thus far, we have considered the abuser's separation from his feeling self and his consequent need to construct a mental picture or ideal image of himself. What happens to all those painful feelings that *must not exist*? As we will see, they are projected upon his partner.

As time passes, the typical abuser is more and more unwilling to face himself and the pain of his feelings. His anger, fear, and self-loathing grow in a secret hidden part of himself and, since he hides this part of himself from himself, he is unable to recognize the source of these feelings. When they do surface, their source, to him, is his partner. This is projection.

Through this projection, he will accuse his partner of all that he does, and blame her for all the abuse that she suffers. She then becomes as he once was, wounded and without a witness to her wounding.

To the abuser, his partner is an extension of himself. When he sees her, he is reminded of his own dark feelings, his own vulnerability—the feelings that "must not exist," the feelings that must be controlled. Consequently, his partner becomes the object of his control and this control becomes her oppression.

To paraphrase Matthew Fox in the film *The Burning Times*, where there is oppression there is projection and out of projection comes denial.

Deep down, the abuser fears his abandoned feeling child within as if it were too awful to ever be accepted. This feeling of awfulness seems, however, not to come from him, but from his partner. Many partners said that when they told their mates that they felt hurt, their mates reacted with accusations such as, "Now you're saying I'm an awful person" or "Now you're attacking me." This is projection. A nonabusive mate would express deep concern, and would apologize, or would talk over the matter with empathy and understanding.

Imagine, if you will, one whose entire psychological orientation is based upon venting the rage of his feeling self, establishing a sense of power through Power Over, bolstering his ideal image—his mental construction of who he is—and defending himself from all knowledge of what he is doing by projecting his feelings onto his partner. This is what the abuser does.

His life becomes a battle against the one who carries his projection. From his stance she, like his feeling self, must not exist. He cannot see her for who she is, nor can he see her reality.

Let us consider verbal abuse in the light of what we now know about the abuser's closed-off feeling self, his ideal image, his projection, and his denial. It becomes evident that every abuse is an attempt by the abuser to *defend* himself from his inner child's feelings of anger, fear and helplessness, and to *protect* himself from the knowledge of what he is doing.

With this in mind, let us briefly review the categories of verbal abuse. And, from this perspective, we may see that all who seek Power Over do so to defend and protect themselves from their own repressed feelings of Personal Powerlessness.

VERBAL ABUSE AS A DEFENSE AND PROTECTION

Withholding enables the abuser to dominate his partner while keeping his ideal image intact. Indeed, to reveal a thought would give the enemy the advantage or perhaps subject him to scrutiny. His ideal image is too fragile a construction to risk such exposure. To respond with interest to his partner would be just as threatening. Such a response would suggest equality, obliterating the abuser's stance of superiority. Without a stance of superiority for protection, the abuser's feelings of powerlessness that must not be felt might be felt.

The abuser who chooses to withhold feels more in control and more powerful if he can remain distant from his partner and, consequently, keep her at bay and yearning. He may also experience a heightened sense of power if his partner's enthusiasm is dampened by his coldness. He seeks this Power Over in order to protect and defend himself from his own feelings of inadequacy.

Likewise, the abuser defends himself against his overwhelming feelings of powerlessness by countering his partner. When he declares himself to be right and his partner to be wrong, he believes himself to be the winner—more powerful and in control.

To say "I think" or "I believe" or "My view is" would remove the possibility of winning over and would open up the possibility of two differing views or experiences both being OK. The abuser cannot tolerate this because, if the partner has a different view from him, he is no longer in control. He has an overwhelming need to control his partner because she carries his projection. If he does not feel that he is in control, his entire reality is shaken.

The abuser gives himself permission to act out his repressed feelings and, at the same time, protects his ideal image by discounting the effects of his abusive behavior. Discounting is a primary defense.

Blocking and diverting are other defenses by which the abuser controls the interpersonal reality. By totally avoiding the topic at hand, he avoids any exploration of the reality of his behavior. Consequently, he maintains his ideal image and alleviates his hidden feelings of powerlessness. The need to control the conversation and hence the outcome may be so intense that some abusers will say with angry apprehension, "I don't see where this conversation is going! So just drop it!"

Accusing and blaming are defenses and significant symptoms of projection. The abuser avoids responsibility for his behavior and maintains his ideal image by declaring his partner guilty and responsible for his feelings. For example, when he attacks her, "it is because of her." In this way he "justifies" the abuse.

Another way the abuser attempts to defend himself against his hidden feelings of inferiority and powerlessness is by criticizing and judging. By declaring his superiority and "rightness" he reinforces both his ideal image and his entire defense system.

Abuse disguised as a joke is a way of winning which gives the abuser a feeling of Power Over. It is a covert hostile attack, denied by the ready-made accusation, "you can't take a joke." This accusation blames the victim and leaves the abuser feeling one up and therefore more powerful. It is a no-risk potshot. The damage is done before the partner can see it coming. "Winning" is assured and the enemy—the projection—is put down once more.

Trivializing, undermining, threatening, and name calling are all defenses against repressed feelings of inadequacy and powerlessness. They are power plays designed by the abuser to denigrate and diminish his partner (his projection).

When the abuser's projection is pervasive, he treats his partner as if she were an extension of himself—the glove on his hand—under his control, there to follow orders. As long as he maintains control of his projection, he feels defended and protected from his own feelings.

By forgetting, the abuser denies responsibility for his behavior while acting out his hostility. In this way he protects his ideal image and maintains his defenses.

All forms of abuse deny the hurt inner child and the acting out of its hostility. The abuser's denial perpetuates his identification with his ideal image, maintains his projection upon his partner, and is a means of avoiding responsibility for his behavior and for its consequences.

Unless he is willing to look into himself, he will not perceive his lack. If he does look into himself, he will confront his own "beast in the jungle"—a life spent, not in living, but in keeping his feelings at bay. Unless he actively seeks personal change through the hard work of therapy, he will, to some degree, have lived a nonlife and have been, to some degree, only an idea of himself. This is his own great personal tragedy.

CHAPTER XVI

About Therapy—And for the Therapist

I experience inspiration from the steps that people take to dispossess perpetrators of their authority, the steps that people take in reclaiming the territories of their lives, in the refashioning of their lives, in having "the last say" about who they are.
— *Michael White*

THERAPEUTIC SUPPORT

I believe that you are the expert on your own experience. I don't believe in privileged knowledge—experts who can tell you how you should be or what is true for you. I do believe a therapist or counselor can assist you if she or he can support you in bringing forth new awareness and new strength. A therapist who supports your process of "seeing the difference"—that is, discriminating between what you have been told about yourself and your own truth about yourself—is most helpful. In addition, a good therapist can assist you in discovering and strengthening your inner resources so that you can make your life more the way you want it to be—all at your own pace.

This chapter addresses therapy primarily in the context of women's experiences of abuse—not because some women are not abusive toward men in relationships, but because almost all of the thousands of cases I have learned about have been heterosexual couple relationships in which men were attempting to control women through verbal abuse. In cases where men suffered this disparagement, their confusion and attempts to resolve the issue were very similar to the partners' experiences in this book. They, too, expressed relief in knowing that they weren't "crazy." The fact that they were reading about women's experiences, not men's, was of no consequence to them.

If you are a therapist reading this chapter first, you will need to know that throughout this book, the word "abuser" describes "the person in the incident or incidents who perpetrates the abuse." The word "abuse" describes those behaviors that attempt to diminish or violate another person, including that person's interests, actions, creations, and so forth. When I use the words "verbally abusive relationship," I am talking about a relationship of oppressor to oppressed in contradistinction to one in which two people are related in mutuality and interdependence.

THERAPY

Therapeutic methods have developed over the past hundred years in the context of the patriarchal and hierarchical assumptions of Western culture. With this in mind, and with the understanding that therapeutic practice is a process in evolution, I present some ideas and views intended to support both therapists and general readers confronting verbal abuse issues.

My perspective is formed by my familiarity with thousands of cases of verbal abuse, by numerous reports and descriptions of therapeutic encounters regarding verbal abuse issues, by systems theory, and by the writings of, and conversations with, therapists who practice therapy from what is called the narrative perspective. If you are interested in more information on narrative therapy than is contained in this chapter, please check the expanded bibliography in this new edition for books by narrative therapists.

In the therapeutic interaction, I do not believe that the therapist should take a neutral position. Nor do I suggest that a therapist take sides with one person against another person. I suggest, instead, that the therapist take the side of change.

I recommend narrative therapy because it is nonhierarchical and takes into account the nature of living systems. In addition, it is based on constructivist theory, a theory that take the view that our identity or self-description is, in part at least, developed through the "stories" we hear about ourselves. In this way we "construct" our identity out of our social milieu.

A constructivist perspective may be employed effectively by therapists to encourage positive change within those who verbally abuse. Partners and former partners of verbal abusers who seek clarity and therapeutic support benefit from its nondirective and respectful approach. If you have therapeutic issues other than those of dealing with verbal abuse, such as a biochemical imbalance, you and your therapist need to decide together your best overall treatment.

Understanding what verbal abuse is can help in the recognition of other abusive behaviors. For instance, a sexually abused child will usually be coerced verbally. A person experiencing emotional pain or mental anguish from encounters with their mate may be able to identify and name what has occurred if they recognize that what has been said to them, or the way they have been treated, is in fact abusive.

If you are a therapist who sees couples or individuals who have been or are presently in verbally abusive relationships, I am sure that their emotional and physical safety is of paramount concern. For this reason as well as for the valuable information they offer, I strongly recommend that, if you haven't already done so, you take part in a training session for volunteers at either a women's shelter or a men's program associated with a women's shelter. Even if you do not decide to work as a volunteer, you will have new information that you can take into your counseling practice.

The domestic violence volunteer training programs and the associated men's programs can be very informative as to the problems people encounter in verbally abusive relationships. They also serve as an introduction to the practical and cultural difficulties people confront in their efforts to escape abuse. In addition they often demonstrate the difficulty some people have in taking responsibility for and giving up their abusive behaviors.

Both verbal abuse and battering are Power Over tactics. An understanding of battering contributes to the recognition of verbal abuse. Conversely, and of real importance, an understanding of verbal abuse enables battered women to recognize that battering has nothing to do with them. They're not to blame. Of course, "understanding" in no way sanctions any abuse.

Simply put, verbal and physical abuse are the same thing in different forms. They are Power Over tactics. For this reason I believe that a verbal abuser benefits from participating in a men's program. This is a powerful addition to therapy even if no battering is involved. Also, *if abuse is even a possibility, it is important for a therapist to see the partner and the abuser separately.*

The people who run men's programs and women's shelters usually know a great deal about verbal abuse. For instance, the

181

MANALIVE (Men Allied Nationally Against Living In Violent Environments) program in Napa, California, along with MAWS (the Marin Abused Women's Services) in San Rafael, California, contributed much information to *Verbal Abuse Survivors Speak Out* (Adams 1993), describing many behaviors related to the categories of verbal abuse in this book.

THE INFLUENCE OF PATRIARCHY

We still live in a patriarchal culture that construes women to be subordinate to men. I used to think, when I was very young, that patriarchy was a term for old men's ideas—ideas like "women shouldn't vote." (Wasn't that verbal abuse?) I thought that patriarchy was about "how it was in the old days." But now I see that patriarchy—a system of erroneous and dehumanizing beliefs about men and women—still has a tremendous influence in our culture and throughout the world. This is not to say that a verbal abuser may not be under other influences (paranoia, for instance).

The therapist may help a person see how patriarchy has influenced his or her life. Discussing beliefs about power, entitlements, having the final say, being the authority in another's life versus being one's own authority, being in charge of another person, and so forth can help the abuser see how patriarchy has taught oppression.

In a very general way, the following example explains how patriarchy can influence a relationship—even create a "non-relationship" under the disguise of a "relationship." Each time a woman says "no" to verbal abuse from her mate—saying, for example, "I don't want to be ordered around," or "I don't want to be told how to do what I do," she challenges patriarchy. The abuser in the interaction, if under the influence of patriarchy, will hear her statement as a challenge to himself (not to patriarchy) and may believe that he must fight her (not patriarchy). He may even assume "She's asking for a fight." The partner, of course, is only asking not to be abused, not to be ordered, and not to be criticized. The partner is seeking a better and closer relationship. Her mate, in this example, is seeking a "win." He has given himself up to patriarchal ideas—in a sense becoming a friend to patriarchy rather than a friend to his partner.

Alan Jenkins (1990) states, "Many abusive men do not regard themselves as having sexist or gender-stereotyped attitudes regarding women or children. They see themselves as egalitarian and fair in their dealings with family members and often feel quite powerless, even regarding their partners as oppressive, controlling and unfair."

When the abuser sees himself as the "victim," he invites his partner to see herself as the culprit. "If I'd just said it differently, he wouldn't have put me down, yelled at me, ordered me." He invites her to join him in a nonsensical and patriarchal view of things—one that exonerates him and makes her responsible for his behavior.

Jenkins also states, "Male abusers may range from quiet, passive men who tend to withdraw from conflict to domineering patriarchs who engage in frequent displays of power and status. Gender-prescribed patterns of exaggerated entitlement and social-emotional avoidance and reliance are evident, however, in both of these extremes."

IDENTIFYING AND NAMING THE "PROBLEM"

Counselors and therapists may have difficulty identifying the dynamics of oppression when a couple present themselves for counseling to "improve the relationship," to "have a better relationship," because they "can't get along," or because they "have been having fights lately."

The same difficulty can occur when a woman comes into counseling by herself because she feels "depressed," is "unhappy about her relationship," or is having "trouble understanding" her mate.

It is not unusual for a therapist to see a couple every week for months and not know that the couple has a verbally abusive relationship. Sometimes no one recognizes the problem. Sometimes both parties, if they recognize it at all, minimize it, and sometimes the abused partner is afraid to mention the abuse for fear of being abused even more.

Likewise, some therapists may not be aware of battering relationships. Sometimes the battered partner is afraid to reveal the incidents. Women have told me that if they said anything about being hit, they "knew" they would be beaten up when they got home or even on the way home. On the other hand, some women didn't recognize that "being hit" by their mate constituted a battering relationship! They thought that once they got into counseling, they would discover "what's wrong," make changes to "what's wrong," and then they wouldn't be hit.

"What's wrong" is of course "what's wrong," that is: the abuse. Whether abuse is verbal or physical, it's the *problem*.

Many traditional therapists are trained to look for pathology, to view the person as the problem and themselves as the experts on the problem (located in the person). Some believe that they have objective knowledge of the person and that what they deem is right for him or her *is* right, regardless of what the person thinks or feels.

Some therapists are directive, believing that they know what you *should* do, or how you *should* be—but your own insight is far more meaningful than someone else's. Changes that are inner-directed, based on your own insight, are also more enduring. Directive and pathologizing therapy takes a one-up position. In effect, it says, "I have expert knowledge that you don't have and therefore I have power over you, so I can confront you, direct you, tell you what to do." The abuse of power in the "therapeutic" relationship is an outcome of therapy based in Reality I.

A man who said he verbally abused his wife wrote to me saying, "We went to couples' counseling for years and verbal abuse was never identified by our therapist." Many women wrote that abuse took place in front of their therapist and their therapist said nothing about it. A number of women said that they experienced abuse *from* their therapist! "You're equally responsible!"—"It takes two!"—"Will you two just quit fighting!"

While these stories are not indicative of most therapeutic encounters, they are common enough to warrant a look at the dynamics of abusive relationships. It seems that for some therapists, learning about Power Over tactics and oppression in relationships was neither a part of their training nor a part of their life experience.

If a therapist is blind to the effects of culture and patriarchy on some relationships, she or he may believe that a verbally abused woman will no longer be abused if she simply becomes more independent and self-assertive. Those therapists who believe that "if you change, he'll change" fail to recognize personal autonomy. They use a "model" for the relationship that no longer serves. For example, sometimes therapists trained in *family* systems view the relationship as if it were a biological system. "If one member (part) of the system changes the other will change." This is neither a useful nor an accurate description of a relationship in which one person seeks to gain and maintain power over the other. On the other hand, in a relationship based upon mutuality such a model might serve, given that *both* parties would be inclined to accommodate the other's requests.

A systemic approach to therapy such as the narrative approach recognizes autonomy. Systems theory makes it quite clear that human beings are autonomous and interdependent living systems. In a similar way all "parts" of an ecological system are both autonomous and interdependent.

We express our autonomy by exercising our freedom of choice. A person may choose to hear the other and to respond, or not to hear the other and not to respond. That is: if you change, your mate may choose *not* to change. If, for example, you are put down and you say, "I don't want you to talk to me that way," your abuser can choose not to respond to your request and may continue the abusive behavior exactly as it was before. Alternatively, the abuser can choose *to* respond. But *how* he responds is again his choice. He may respond by increasing the abuse or changing the type of abuse, or he may respond by choosing to stop the abuse.

Generally, a narrative or Reality II therapy locates the problem of verbal abuse in cultural practices (internalized in the individual) that condone Power Over, entitlement, and assumed superiority of one person over another person. These practices are inadvertently passed on in the family.

A narrative therapist sees the person's life as being framed in a cultural story, and sees problems occurring when people go to extremes to fit themselves into a preformulated cultural prescription. The therapist invites people to make new distinctions and to see alternative ways of being. Narrative therapy does not imply the one-upmanship of some traditional approaches but is, instead, a therapeutic stance of collaboration and mutuality between client and therapist.

THE THERAPEUTIC INTERVIEW

By asking questions, the therapist may bring forth from each individual insight into the nature of the problem and all that supports it. Describing the problem, naming it and locating its support in culturally prescribed gender descriptions can begin to allow it to be seen as "the problem" as opposed to the person or persons being seen as "the problem."

Following is a very small sample of some of the kinds of questions that invite people to see the difference between Power Over behaviors that prevent true "relationship" and supportive behaviors that develop that "relationship."

A woman may meet with a therapist and say something like, "I'm not happy. I've been feeling depressed lately. I can't seem to get along with my husband."

The therapist can foster new insight by asking such questions as:

What happens when you feel that you and he aren't getting along?

Was there a time when you felt like you were getting along?

What do you notice that's different now?

Can you tell me a little bit more about that?

Can you tell me how he expresses interest in you—your thoughts, opinions, plans, and so forth?

What has the last week been like for you?

What have you heard him say about that?

If verbal abuse is identified as the problem, the partner, *not the abuser*, might be asked to consider the following questions:

How has verbal abuse affected your life?

Has verbal abuse taken a good deal of your time?

How often does verbal abuse occur?

Did verbal abuse affect your life five or ten years ago?

If verbal abuse continued in the direction it's going (appearing more often or causing more trouble), what do you think your life would be like five or ten years from now?

If you continued to try not to have it happen by being careful of what you say in the future, what kinds of things do you think would be safe to say?

Can you see how amazed I am that you have done so well under these circumstances?

A therapist can support an abuser in gaining insights into his own behavior, by inviting him to explore his beliefs about himself and the relationship in the context of cultural prescriptions for "manhood" and how these ideas conflict with the reality of a relationship.

To a narrative therapist, there are few interactions between couples that are not influenced by patriarchy. If there is an abuse of power in a relationship, a narrative therapist would view the responsibility for the abuse of power as lying in the hands of the person abusing the power.

A narrative approach would invite the abuser to

1. Recognize the abuse as abuse.

2. Position himself against it.

3. Accept total responsibility for stopping it.

The therapist would invite the abuser to consider the beliefs and ideas he entertains that support his behavior, and the effect they have on his partner and on the relationship. If the problem is identified as verbal abuse, the therapist would pose questions that externalize patriarchal ideas about male dominance. Following are some examples:

> How have you responded to your partner's resistance to your direction?
>
> How has your desire to direct her affected your relationship?
>
> What happens when your partner expresses an opinion that you don't share?
>
> Has the idea that you should be in charge brought your partner closer to you?
>
> When the desire to "win" over her (takes you by surprise) (gets the upper hand) how might you put it down?
>
> Who will prevail, you or the desire to dominate?
>
> What might happen if dominance prevails?
>
> How do you feel about yourself when you prevail? How did you manage to keep dominance at bay?

These questions shift the locus of responsibility for the abuse to the abuser and invite him to take responsibility for his behavior.

It is helpful to invite a person who abuses to recall a time when he didn't choose to exert power over his partner, but might have, and to discuss the meaning and the significance of that exception.

What was his behavior in other contexts—for example, in the initial stages of courting his partner or at the office with his boss? In this way he may be able to "see" the difference between his behaviors. He may come to his own insight that his abusive behavior with his partner cannot be excused by a supposed relational deficit due to his family history.

A narrative therapist would have the abuser differentiate his intentions (trying to keep his relationship with his wife) from his actions (abuse to maintain control of the relationship). The goal here is to support the abuser in constructing a healthy sense of self-worth, one that is not based on power over, coercion, one-upmanship, or a claim of superiority.

The therapist can invite the abuser to discuss his understanding of mutuality. "What does mutuality mean to you? Do you think it means the same thing to your partner?"

When the abuser recognizes the damaging influence of patriarchy on the relationship and wants to remove patriarchy from the relationship, he can be invited to make a stand against it, to be alert and vigilant and to put it down when he senses its presence. He can be invited to openly explore the ways in which patriarchy challenges his preferred (nonabusive) way of being.

These steps take time and cannot even begin until the abuse is recognized and the abuser, hopefully with the support of a men's program, accepts responsibility for his behavior.

If the abuser denies the abuse or responsibility for it ("She had it coming! She made me do it!"), his partner may move out and he may move on to become abusive in his next relationship.

Some abusive men, even as they court a new partner, continue to pursue the "one that got away." They can be invited to see that these ongoing attempts to "get" her are not about relationship. They are about patriarchal ideas of possession and ownership.

Even when an abuser has acknowledged his abusive behavior, he may find that it takes great effort and much time to stop it. And even when he seems to have stopped it, a verbally abused partner may be too traumatized to even entertain the idea of rebuilding the relationship with him.

The therapist would invite him to both accept that patriarchy had destroyed the relationship and to let go of it without blaming the partner. *Ultimately abusers must stop abusing because they do not want to be abusive people.*

DENIAL

Denial can block all efforts to stop verbal abuse in a relationship. Denial is like an automatic defense mechanism and is fully defined in psychological literature. For our purposes, a simple way to describe it is to say that the abuser thinks "I haven't done anything wrong (abusive)" and then believes his thought, despite the evidence.

The following example illustrates just how intense denial can be: A therapist in practice for many years found that he was working with men who came to him for help in dealing with their violence against their partners. The therapist decided to go to a men's program. He wanted to watch how it worked, and he hoped to learn some techniques that he could use with the men who came to him. He wanted to help them to take responsibility for their behavior and to overcome their abusive ways. While attending the men's program he came to the shocking realization that he, himself, was a batterer.

This man had the courage to tell his story to the world on a national television show. He presented a clear picture of how total denial can be, and also a clear picture of how a person's image can fool, not only the world, but also himself.

Denial of abuse is extremely confusing to the partner of an abuser. The partner is twice abused—once by the abuse and once by its denial. Needless to say, therapists need to be very aware of this. Many people who have suffered from verbal abuse feel an almost overwhelming need to hear their abuser acknowledge that the abuse is unjustified—that it is abuse. It doesn't always happen. However, some abusers break through their denial by reading a transcript of what they have said. For the first time they come to the realization that they have, indeed, said "those things."

An abuser usually expresses shock when he recognizes his behavior. And often the first thing he says is, "I'm an awful person." (I am always amazed that so many abusers say exactly the same thing!) By having externalized patriarchal prescriptions of superiority, dominance, and nonresponsibility, as discussed earlier, the abuser can come to the realization that he is *a person* and his behavior is *a choice*. If he clings to the idea that something within him—his "awfulness" or his "past"—is the *cause* of his behavior, he may escape accountability, and instead of blaming his behavior on his partner may now blame it on his "awfulness"—his very nature!

Although the "past" or the "culture" help to bring us some understanding of what supports abusive behavior, responsibility for abuse rests with the abuser.

John Stoltenberg says, "This search for an explanation of men's abusiveness and violence sometimes borders on being a search for an apology: 'How could he be any different, poor thing?—look how he grew up!' Thus does men's evasion of ethical accountability get therapeutic validity and academic respectability."

A NONTHERAPEUTIC ENCOUNTER

Jill, married to Jack, sent me the following letter after reading the first edition of this book.

It all began when I found your book. There it was in black and white, the problem I was dealing with, for the first time so clearly defined. My heart soared. I had found validation of what I had known to be true inside but could not express.

So many sources I had read suggested that the problem in an unhappy relationship was the woman, that she was just too caring or too involved. I believed all this without even realizing it. Taking all the responsibility for the relationship and my husband's behavior was what a woman was "supposed to do."

When Jack would start blaming and accusing me, I would patiently try to explain to him, "No, that's not what I said, not what I did." I thought I could get him to see what he was doing. I believed that he was just ignorant, wounded from childhood abuses. I thought that if I was a "real" woman, I could get him to see the light—to want to stop being abusive. [Note: This is patriarchy influencing a woman's thinking.]

No matter how I tried, he continued to abuse me. I felt that I was failing as a woman and as a person.

But now, everything was different. I realized the issue wasn't my not being understanding enough, my not being able to explain things well enough, my not being tolerant enough, nor was it his tortured family background or the relationship itself. It was verbal abuse.

For the first time I knew I was not to blame for the abuse. I wasn't responsible for any part of it. He was the perpetrator. He owned the problem. With this validation came the beginning of my empowerment.

When, as was his custom, he entered my room with his blaming and accusing, I, armed with new knowledge and self-assurance, simply said to him, "Cut it out, Jack. Leave me alone."

A look of sudden shock immobilized him in the doorway. For the first time he was stopped from his verbal abuse.

He left the room only to come back later in a very strange mood. "When you told me that, it was like you called me on my game," he said.

I did not show what I was thinking inside, but I was shocked. I thought to myself, "What! We've been married eleven years and all that time you've been playing a game with me?! Our whole marriage has been nothing but a power-over game to you! You weren't the innocent victim unintentionally passing on the same abuse you'd been given, you were deliberately trying to gain control over me!?"

He went on, "I don't want to live like this. I want to get help."

That moment opened up an opportunity for change. A good therapist was crucial. My husband could slip back into abusing any minute. He agreed to therapy. I knew a great therapist for individuals. But to make a long story short, he wasn't a great therapist for couples. He was gender-blind and therefore power-blind. He didn't understand the dynamics of verbally abusive relationships and he saw verbal abuse as less of a problem than physical abuse. And just as bad, he ended up victimizing me, unintentionally I'm sure.

Initially Jack had accepted full responsibility for verbally abusing me but our therapist kept Sherlock Holmsing for weaknesses in both of us in order to make "sense" of the problem. And, he wouldn't read about my experiences, even though they were all highlighted in the book that, by then, I'd given him. Instead, he conveyed an attitude that came across as, "How dare we, the sick people in his eyes, try to give him, the superior mental health professional, any insight into our problem. Insight was his job, not ours."

He devised a behavioral plan for my husband whereby I was to take half the responsibility. Immediately I questioned him. Why was I expected to fix my husband's problem? What did he do in the case of a couple where the man was physically abusing his partner? Would he expect the partner to be partly responsible for a problem that wasn't hers?

"No," he told me. "In that case you would separate the couple and give the woman support and give the man therapy that would focus on his violence."

"This dynamic," I told him, "was not different. So why are you forcing me to be partly responsible for a problem that is not mine? This is gender bias."

"Jill," he told me, "you're talking about physical violence. This is only verbal abuse. It is not the same thing. Jack is verbally abusive, but you're just too sensitive. Normally you should be able to let the stuff he does just roll off your back."

We agreed to disagree, but unfortunately my husband, who had come in accepting one hundred percent responsibility for his abuse, gladly gave it up. He had found a new ally in his efforts to shift his responsibility onto me. Needless to say, his abuse of me escalated horrifically. It seemed that my husband felt justified, even mandated, by the therapeutic world.

I never expected that I would be abused by the psychologist I had enlisted to help, but that is exactly what happened.

FINDING A THERAPIST

When I consult with people about the dynamics of their interpersonal communication and the nature of verbal abuse, I support them in becoming clear about what they are hearing and what they are saying. Then, if they request ongoing therapeutic support, I refer them to a therapist who understands the issues around verbal abuse.

Many therapists—psychiatrists, psychologists, MFCCs (Marriage, Family, and Child Counselor) and LCSWs (Licensed Clinical Social Worker)—use my books, referring them to their clients. I know because I receive letters that say something like, "My therapist [or doctor] recommended your book and really understands what I'm going through." But the writers don't always tell me who the therapist is. If you have a therapist you think is great, please don't hesitate to pass your recommendation on to me, including his or her name, address, and phone number.

When I receive a call, letter, or e-mail from someone asking, "Do you know a therapist in my area who understands verbal abuse?" I am glad to refer the person to therapists who have taken one of my workshops or who have been referred to me by others. But I make no guarantees.

If you are looking for therapeutic support, I suggest that you interview as many therapists as necessary until you find one who feels right for you.

I would reject:

- Therapists who do not see that verbal abuse is an act of violence just as physical abuse is. (They lack training.)

- Therapists who do not have an understanding of patriarchy, power, and gender. (They will be blind to the abuse.)

- Therapists who hold the partner in any way responsible for the abuser's pervasive pattern of abuse. (Their therapeutic orientation would end up abusing the partner.)

- Therapists who do not take to heart the partner's experience, because it is presented in a book such as this one. (They would be invested in privileging their "expert" knowledge over valuing the partner's experience.)

- Therapists whose therapeutic stance does not open space for new ways of being in a respectful, collaborative way.

It's your choice. You are the expert on your own experience!

CHAPTER XVII

Children and Verbal Abuse

What would it be like if all of us regarded our children
as children of God—which we could do, after all?
— *Alice Miller*

Many questions surround the issue of children and verbal abuse.
For example:

How can I encourage high self-esteem in my child?

What do I say to a child who has experienced verbal abuse
from another child or from an adult?

What do I say to my child when he [she] calls me names?

How can my child best handle verbal abuse from peers?

What do I say to my child if I have left a relationship in
which I experienced verbal abuse?

How can I keep myself separate when I share care of my
child with my former spouse?

There are no perfect answers to these questions. The answers
presented here are suggestions—models of effective ways to communicate that are meant to assist you in the process of honoring,
respecting, and protecting your child from the emotional and
mental harm of verbal abuse.

ENCOURAGING YOUR CHILD'S SELF-ESTEEM
When a parent faces a stressful situation and their child needs attention, the urgencies of the moment can invite a hasty response.

Even when they have time to think, a parent may overlook obvious solutions or actions because his or her mind is in turmoil.

For this reason, it is helpful for parents to remind themselves of the need to treat their child with goodwill and respect, even when they feel stressed.

When respect becomes the context for what you say, what you say is more likely to convey respect.

Courses in parenting are given in most cities, and many books on raising children are available. Sometimes it is difficult to choose between different philosophies. When you choose books on parenting and child raising, I believe the most essential criterion is that they foster respect for the child. If you give your children love and attention, are empathetic to their feelings, and are honest with them and encourage their independence, you will, in most cases, see them grow up to be loving, attentive, empathetic, honest, and independent adults.

Sometimes peer pressure or abuse from outside the home and so forth can influence the child to act out in undesirable ways. Don't be quick to blame yourself. You can only do your best. When in doubt, seek outside help through parenting classes, counselors, and/or other parents you admire.

Communicating Confidence

I believe that one of the most effective ways to impart confidence is to allow the child to meet his or her own needs as soon as the child shows an ability to do so. Parents can say:

Do you want to try using this spoon yourself?

I'll wait while you tie your shoes.

Are you ready to make your own peanut butter sandwich?

Here is the way to use the washer.

Communicating Appreciation

Children respond to appreciation. They are born good, curious, and spontaneous. Every child has unique talents and interests. As a parent, your job is to give your child the attention he or she needs. Noticing what the child likes—music, dancing, running, bright colors, quiet times, sports, and so on—and introducing and fostering the child's interests, even though they are not your own, brings forth from the child the childs own unique self. Following are ways of expressing appreciation:

What a beautiful picture.

Tell me about the book you like best.

It looks like you took extra time to make that.

Do you need some extra time to finish that?

I really appreciate your being quiet and waiting until I finished talking.

Communicating Limits

Good communication includes communicating limits to your child. Children feel safe and cared for when parents set limits for them. When they become adults, they set their own limits. They are best able to do this when they learn how during their childhood.

You can set limits for your child while still validating his or her feelings. For instance, it is natural for children to want to stay up past bedtime or to want things they can't have, but there are limits to their endurance and to the number and kinds of possessions they can have. You, as the parent, should encourage them to realize this. For example:

I hear you. You want to stay up, but now it's bedtime for five-year-olds. After you're ready, we'll read a story.

I can see that you want to watch that on TV, but that's not a kids' show. Let's pick out something else.

That's not okay.

When you're screaming I can't hear you. Let me hear your words.

Let's talk about it.

Tell me what you want.

No, I'm not buying any toys today.

I'd like you to have that, too, but I don't have the money for it.

Communicating Choices

Whenever possible, children should be given the opportunity to choose. It takes extra effort on the part of the parent—it's easier to say, "You're wearing this, like it or not." But if your child learns early on that she or he can make choices and take responsibility for them, your child will be better able to make good choices in life. Following are some examples of ways that you can present your child with the opportunity to make choices:

Do you want corn or peas?

Both your white top and your yellow top look nice with these pants—which do you want to wear?

This is the school menu. Do you want to buy lunch or take your own?

Is there anything you want to do this school year, like sports or the photography club?

Who would you like to invite to your birthday party?

WHEN CHILDREN HEAR VERBAL ABUSE

Sometimes, even while trying to protect a child, a parent may lose sight of just how to respect the child's feelings. For example, a woman wrote, "In the past I had a grandfather who yelled at me and berated me. My own parents told me to not let Grandpa bother me—to just ignore him. I was really happy when he passed away."

In a situation like this, the child needs to hear, "What he just did [said] is not okay. Come with me while I tell him." The abuser needs to hear, "What you said to Mary [or John] is not okay. I really don't want her [him] to hear this kind of talk again."

If you are abused for speaking up, take yourself and your child out of harm's way, again acknowledging your child's feelings ("I know it hurts when he talks mean") and reiterating to your child the fact that that kind of talk is not okay.

If your child is yelled at or put down in any way, she or he needs your support. Sometimes a parent may inadvertently teach a child to put up with abuse. It is sometimes helpful to ask yourself, "Is there anything in what I've said that minimizes the abuse?"

If a child is told by a parent, "She [he] didn't mean that," the child's experience is invalidated and his or her pain discounted. The abuse is minimized and the child is taught to tolerate it.

Minimizing abuse is something most people *are* taught. To say, "Forget it. He was just having a bad day" may seem like a way to make the pain go away, but it just leaves the hurt inside. And it's crazymaking. (Does having a bad day make abuse okay?)

When you acknowledge your child's feelings and respond to verbal abuse, you validate the child's experience. And you are the all-important sympathetic witness. In this way you teach your child appropriate responses to verbal abuse and help your child to honor his or her own feelings.

On the other hand, teaching your child to pretend that words don't hurt (something males especially are taught) doesn't do anything good for the child. It even makes children doubt themselves.

Depending on your child's age and to whom she or he needs to respond, your child needs to learn appropriate responses to verbal abuse such as those covered in this book. Even an older child needs emotional support to respond to an adult who verbally abuses. "I'll stand by you" may be all the child needs to hear.

Children learn to abuse from adults and from each other. One of the most effective responses a child can make to a peer who puts him [her] down is to say, "That's what YOU say," with a strong emphasis on "you."

This response usually startles the other child and implies "I don't buy it. You said it. You are responsible for what you say."

Sometimes a child is verbally abused while visiting a parent after separation or divorce. I recently talked with a woman whose son would come back from visiting his father appearing very upset. When asked what was wrong, his standard reply would be, "If I tell you, even if you say you won't tell, he'll find out." Clearly, this is a serious problem. The child is suffering and feels too threatened to confide the incident.

If the parent cannot gain the child's confidence, outside intervention—a family friend, relative, or counselor who could become the child's confidant—would be of real value.

WHEN CHILDREN VERBALLY ABUSE
If you hear a child indulging in verbal abuse, you might try some of the following responses. They are appropriate to different circumstances and to different ages. See how they fit with your needs:

"That kind of talk is not okay."

"I don't want to hear that kind of talk from you."

"That kind of talk doesn't invite me to admire you."

"That's enough of that."

"There'll be no more of that kind of talk in my home."

WHEN PARENTS SEPARATE

Is there anything about your existing relationship that you know is not nurturing or healthy for you and your children and that you hope will go away if ignored?

If a child is abused or is a witness to abuse, the child suffers. A woman said to me, "Staying can hurt the child. It is totally invalid to think that staying in a marriage 'for the sake of the children' has any merit whatsoever. It is extremely detrimental. Whether the abuse shifts to the child or the child just unconsciously absorbs the mechanics of an abusive relationship, it is agonizingly painful in the long run." This woman was speaking from her own experience.

As children grow older in abusive circumstances, they may act out their frustration, pain, and confusion or try to obliterate it with drugs or other self-destructive means. They may even try suicide. Girls may be more inclined to withdraw, boys to become aggressive. If children are not raised in a peaceful and loving home, having both parents in the home does not make it healthier.

While children need both parents to treat them with respect and dignity and to attend equally to their needs, this isn't always possible. It is important to know that children can be better off in a nonabusive single-parent home than in one in which abuse takes place.

If you separate from your spouse, it is important that your child be allowed to express his or her feelings about that to you. A child may say "I hate you" meaning that he or she hates what's happened. Saying "I hate you" is not verbal abuse. It is an intense expression of feeling.

You may hear something like this when you are feeling most vulnerable. Even so, when your child is upset by changes in your relationship, it is important that you recognize his or her feelings. An appropriate response would be, "It sounds like you're angry and you feel bad. I don't blame you. I wish things were different too. I love you." Knowing what to expect can help you to respond in ways that respect your child's feelings.

Leaving an abusive situation, however, can be very difficult if the courts do not take the time to listen to children.

A woman who had left an abusive mate gave me this account of her experience.

I'll never forget my supervisor's voice. "The courts are biased against women," she said, when I told her I'd started my divorce.

I did think I might suffer financially, but I was sure my children would be protected—that the courts would be reasonable when it came to the welfare of these precious ones. To my horror, I was wrong. Absolutely. To say that a mother's worst nightmare came true would be an understatement. What happened to me in the court system was unthinkable.

My two little daughters sleep in my bed tonight, afraid to leave my side. They cry for hours each week when they are forced to leave. My young son returns home to me in states of depression and heightened anxiety. He has nightmares almost every night about a monster coming to take him away. All this at a judge's mandate. All in acquiescence to those who have the dominant voice in the system.

My daughter screams, "Momma don't leave me with daddy . . . . Daddy's mean to me. He hits me. He's not good. He's a bad daddy. Momma don't leave me!"

When I asked her father to consider her fear and pain, he threatened me in front of her, "Don't make me have the courts take these kids away from you."

I am bullied by him and terrified by his abuse. It is no surprise that my little children are also.

Even with evidence of spousal and child abuse, the judge turned my children over to their father for fifty percent of the time. My pleas for compassion for the children fell on deaf ears. Their voices were not even heard.

Their father had bragged to friends how he was going to make me pay for leaving him, laughing while telling his dream of my being so financially drained I would be forced to live in my car while he took control of everything.

I know this because they came to me in shock, warning me of his "craziness."

Today when my children came home one said "Mommy, daddy is going to take our house away. He's mad at you Momma. He's mean to you." I say nothing to them about their father.

The children have become his pawns. Their emotional dev-

astation is of no concern to him. Evidence of his abusive and even criminal behavior is likewise of no concern to the court.

To please the court I had proposed that our children have almost daily visits with their father, but primary residence with me. Though he had rarely spent time interacting with the children, he decided to fight this. He demanded that the children be taken out of their home to live with him half of the time. "That way I won't have to pay her a dime," I overheard him say.

He told the court I was making the children "act up." He insisted I was crazy and wrote pages of lies about me. He was making me pay for leaving him.

The tragedy is that the courts will give a man like this exactly what he wants. And afterwards he will likely abandon his children entirely. The system allows this. Every day it turns children over to sexually perpetrating, drug addicted or emotionally violent abusers. There is no justice here. It's crazy!

My only hope is that when he begins to deal with other people's criminal complaints against him, he will no longer have the energy to punish me.

KEEPING SEPARATE

Many women who leave abusive relationships are re-traumatized each time they see their former mate. Each time their child is picked up or left off, they may see the person who persecuted them. They may even be abused again. A woman said, "You've got a fifty/fifty shot. You don't know whether Jekyll or Hyde will be there."

One solution is to set up a neutral place—a baby-sitter's home or other safe place where your mate can leave the child ten minutes before you are to arrive, or you can leave the child minutes before your mate is to arrive.

STALKING THROUGH THE CHILD

Some partners who leave verbally and sometimes physically abusive relationships report a strange and sad phenomenon. So many women have informed me of this that it deserves to be addressed here.

When an abuser is unable to keep his agreement to put his child's needs first, even when he voices his willingness to do so, he may attempt to gain power over his partner through his child. If he is immersed in Reality I, is closed to the experience of mutuality, and has not dealt with his need for Power Over, the need will still be there. If he hasn't transferred his need to control to a new partner, his former partner may well be "it."

Stalking the mother through the child is accomplished by telling the child something like the following; "I love your mother. I want us all to be together again. If we're to get back together, I need to know what she's doing, where she goes, what she wears, who she talks to, what she says. You can't trust anyone but me."

The child wants everything to be okay. The child wants love. The child cannot know when she or he is being manipulated.

But when children grow up they sometimes know and tell. They tell of being manipulated into spying and making reports. They tell of their confusion. They tell of their mixed feelings of loyalty and guilt and sadness.

The former partners of such abusers say that such stalking of their lives is a living nightmare for themselves and for their children.

If you need to ensure your separateness from a former spouse, your child may benefit from knowing the information that follows. You may read it to your child or make a copy for your child. If you are an educator, therapist, or social worker, you may pass it out to the parents you see.

When Your Parents Live Apart

- Your relationship to each of your parents is separate and special.

- It is okay to say, "I don't want to talk about it," if one of your parents asks you about your other parent.

- It is important to tell your parent, counselor, or an adult you trust about anything that hurts, confuses, or bothers you, even when it is dad or mom you have to talk about.

- It is not a parent's business to know anything about the other parent's life when they are no longer together.

- It is not okay for one parent to ask you details about your other parent's life.

- You do not have to answer a parent's questions about the other parent, as for instance the following: "What is your mom [or dad] doing? Who does she [or he] talk to? What does she [or he] say? What does she [or he] wear?

- You can say, "Never mind."

- You can say, "I don't want to talk about it."

The Verbally Abusive Relationship:
How to Recognize It and How to Respond
by Patricia Evans
Adams Media Corporation, second edition.

Frequently Asked
Questions

1. Is verbal abuse in a relationship part of a power struggle?

I do not use the words "power struggle" in this book, but the idea of abuse being part of a power struggle comes up a lot in popular self-help literature. It deserves discussion because the concept is confusing to a person in a verbally abusive relationship. A power struggle involves two people or groups trying to "win" over or have power over each other. Two football teams are in a power struggle on the field. Two boxers are in a power struggle in the ring. A relationship isn't a football field or a boxing ring.

When a woman in a verbally abusive relationship asks her mate, for instance, not to tell her what to do or not to criticize her, her mate may immediately see this request as a power struggle—a challenge to his "authority" and a dispute to be won.

The partner, on the other hand, usually views her request as a plea for acceptance, love, and freedom from pain—a chance to have a better relationship. She thinks that once the request is heard, her mate will change his behavior, will want to know what is bothering her, will even feel excruciatingly sad for the pain he has inflicted.

2. Am I to be thought of as a victim or as a survivor of verbal abuse?

Many contemporary books discuss the issue of people identifying with being a victim or being a survivor. What does all this mean in the context of verbally abusive relationships, in terms of actual victimization or actual survival?

Becoming aware of the influences of Power Over tactics in the culture and in relationships reduces their influence. Once aware, a person is much less likely to feel like a victim of these tactics and can take empowering steps toward building a life in accord with what she or he wants.

Usually, when a woman recognizes the nature of verbal abuse and its influence on her life she can begin to find a way to gain freedom from abuse. As she does so, the feeling of being victimized fades away.

I believe that when people are "brainwashed" by constant verbal abuse, they are victimized. When they realize that in all cases of verbal abuse, they are being lied to, the negative statements begin to lose their impact. This, of course, is especially true if they are not subject to continuing abuse. For instance, a child growing up completely unaware of Power Over tactics who hears that "A woman's place is in the home," or that "Boys don't cry," and who internalizes this as if it were actually true, is victimized. Recognizing the oppression of these statements, letting go of being able to "have" a relationship with a person seeking power over us, and finding our own truth frees us from the experience of victimization.

When a person who was once abused is freed from the influence of abuse in her life, she has survived abuse. Having survived something—whether it is a forest fire, a sinking ship, or an abusive relationship—does not mean that you need to build your identity around having been victimized or having survived. It simply means that in surviving a difficult situation, you may also have discovered how you did it and you may have something to teach others—for instance, how to avoid forest fires, when to jump ship, or how to avoid a potentially disastrous relationship.

3. Is interrogation a category of verbal abuse?

Interrogation is a form of diversion. If you are asked a question and then you are interrupted with another question, and then, just as you focus on *that* question, you are asked another question, and each question is expressed with urgency, you are being diverted from your train of thought over and over again. One woman who experienced interrogation said, "I felt like my brain was turned into a pretzel. I didn't think of it as abuse. I thought I should try harder to answer the question, or to figure out what he was trying to ask. I wanted to answer his question, but it kept changing. I felt I'd failed. It could take a week to recover, to feel normal again."

4. What is a double message and how does it affect me?
Much confusion in abusive relationships originates with "double messages." The basic double message of a verbally abusive relationship is "I love you" (nice words) and "I don't love you" (abusive words).

One of the most common contexts in which verbal abuse takes place is a marriage or committed relationship. Marriages and committed relationships are thought to be loving relationships. Abuse in this context is crazymaking because it presents a double message. This is home (a safe place). This is where abuse takes place (not a safe place).

When two messages are sent at the same time, the person getting them is "caught" in the middle of two different sets of information. When a violent man said of his relationship with a woman he periodically beat up, "If we had a problem it's because I loved her so much," his statement was crazymaking. Love doesn't create problems. Dominance does.

5. If I am to be accepting of my mate, does that mean I have to accept the things he says to me or the way he treats me?
The hardest thing to accept is the reality of abuse. If a woman is verbally abused, it can become extremely difficult and painful to accept what her own experience is telling her. She may doubt herself and all her experiences. If she also believes that she needs to be accepting of her mate's behavior, she will find it even more difficult to accept her own truth.

Some women believe that the acceptance of their mate's abusive behavior is part of loving their mate. For instance, one abused woman, Nicole Brown, held the confused belief that she should have been more "accepting."

The acceptance of abuse expresses confusion or real fear of physical harm to self or children.

6. Is there such a thing as spiritual abuse?
Yes. Some Power Over people disguise themselves as God. In some cases they tell some persons (women) that they must be subject to the will of other persons (men). The evil of this oppression is touted as "God's will." This is an example of taking the name of God in vain. Sometimes a whole community may be indoctrinated this way, both women and men.

Sometimes a woman who is thus indoctrinated will come to believe that God's will is her husband's will or some other man's will. This very same woman, who would not presume to tell a man he must follow her direction, may not question the fact that someone has told her how to live her life.

When women who, taught to accept this oppression, awaken to the reality of their own spirituality and even discover the history of women's spirituality, they say that they feel freed and at the same time deeply betrayed.

There is something evil in using the idea of "God," which to many people means "Love," to teach oppression. This is undermining to all people everywhere.

7. My husband says he feels abused when I don't take direction from him or wait on him. Is he abused just because he feels abused?

Abuse is the oppression of one person by another. The oppressor may feel abused because he isn't successful in gaining domination of his partner or because his partner resists domination. He may feel diminished in his own eyes, especially if he thinks that being a man means being dominant.

In a similar way, if carried to the extreme, we can surmise that a rapist feels more like a man if he succeeds in raping (taking) a woman and less like a man if he doesn't succeed. This would be in keeping with an internalized and mistaken idea that a woman is an object to be taken and that a real man would take her.

It sounds as though your husband has mistaken you for a servant or even a slave. Possibly he feels like a failure because you don't act like either one of these. It may be easier for him to feel abused by your freedom than to give up his belief that you "should" obey him.

8. Why don't you write about men's experiences of being verbally abused in relationships?

Men are their own best authority on their experience of verbal abuse in relationships and would be the ones best able to describe their experience. I have little if any information on this topic. From what I have heard, however, it seems that men most often experience verbal abuse in the culture at large, especially in regard to establishing one-upsmanship with each other, and in regard to being told they must act in certain ways, and comply with other men's ideas of what it is to be a person in order to be accepted as a man by other men.

9. How do I know when to recognize the covert verbal abuser who tells me what I want to hear to get me hooked? I want to keep my optimism, be open yet guarded, positive yet realistic.

The time to recognize abuse is, of course, the moment it happens, but covert abuse can challenge a woman's discriminatory abilities to the extreme. If he makes comments that hurt but claims they are a joke, you are with an abuser. If your mate isn't willing to listen to your feelings and treats you as if you are less than you are, you are with an abuser. An abusive relationship is more an attitude toward you than a rare moment of anger or irritation over a difference of opinion.

A man told me that one day, as he and his fiancée were driving home from a movie theater, she expressed an opinion different from his about the film they had just seen. For some reason, he said, he got angry and started to raise his voice to her. (He still doesn't understand why he did this.)

They were stopped at a traffic light. His partner said, "I'm hearing abuse from you," stepped out of the car, and left. (And she hadn't even read my books!)

He called out her name several times but she was gone. "She just disappeared into the night," he said.

He felt very shaken. Traffic prevented him from following her. He went home. She hadn't called. Finally, two days later, she appeared.

He never did it again.

10. Isn't it appropriate to keep our focus on refusing to be abused rather than genderizing it?

When it comes to adult-couple relationships, we can't genderize verbal abuse because it already is a gender issue.

11. Do women unconsciously choose abusers to deal with their unresolved issues?

Most women choose mates who court them. Women usually experience an attentive and affectionate person because while he's courting her, his approach to her is conciliatory. However, once he's "gotten" her, if he believes that "now" he has certain entitlements and prerogatives, is somehow superior, is inferior if he shows vulnerability and warmth, is weak if he reveals his own feelings, is born to be in charge of a woman, has no responsibility to build and maintain the relationship, should be the center of her attention and she should do his bidding, his attitude toward her and his treatment of her will change.

This change is most confusing to a woman. She may long remember how he was—and for just as long, hope that he will be that way again.

Bibliography

WORKS CITED

Bach, George R., and Ronald Deutsch. *Stop! You're Driving Me Crazy*. New York: G.P. Putnam's Sons, 1980, p. 16.

Bach, George R., and Herb Goldberg. *Creative Aggression*. New York: Doubleday & Co., 1974, pp. 16, 19, 38.

Fleming, Jennifer Baker. *Stopping Wife Abuse: A Guide to the Emotional, Psychological, and Legal Implications . . . for the Abused Woman and Those Helping Her*. New York: Anchor Books, 1979, pp. 142, 161.

Fulghum, Robert. *All I Really Need To Know I Learned In Kindergarten: Uncommon Thoughts on Common Things*. New York: Random House, Inc., 1989, p. 14.

Horney, Karen. *Our Inner Conflicts: A Constructive Theory of Neurosis*. New York: W.W. Norton and Company, 1992, p. 160.

Jenkins, Alan. *Invitations to Responsibility: The Therapeutic Engagement of Men Who Are Violent and Abusive*. Adelaide, South Australia: Dulwich Centre Publications, 1990, p. 44.

Miller, Alice (trans. Hildegarde and Hunter Hannum). *For Your Own Good: Hidden Cruelty in Child-Rearing and the Roots of Violence*. New York: Farrar, Straus, and Giroux, 1983, p. 159.

—. (trans. Hildegarde and Hunter Hannum). *Thou Shalt Not Be Aware: Society's Betrayal of the Child*. New York: Farrar, Straus, and Giroux, Inc., 1990, p. 97.

—. *The Untouched Key*. New York: Random House, 1990, p. 159.

Paul, Jordan, and Margaret Paul. *Do I Have to Give Up Me to Be Loved by You?* Irvine, Calif.: Compcare Publishers, 1983, p. 39.

Stoltenberg, John. *Refusing to Be a Man: Essays on Sex and Justice*. New York: Meridian, Penguin Books, 1990, p. 202.

White, Michael. *Re-Authoring Lives: Interviews & Essays*. Adelaide, South Australia: Dulwich Centre Publications, 1995, p. 86.

Winn, Denise. *The Manipulated Mind: Brainwashing, Conditioning and Indoctrination.* London: Octagon Press, 1983, p. 103.

FOR FURTHER READING

This list of recommended reading has been selected primarily because these books will support you in taking control of your life. They are action-oriented and may help you to know yourself and your talents better. Many offer step-by-step approaches toward meeting your goals or creating a fulfilling and nurturing life for yourself.

Barnett, O.W., and A.D. LaViolette. *It Could Happen to Anyone: Why Battered Women Stay.* Newbury Park, Calif.: Sage Publications, 1993. This book brings to light the mental anguish and emotional pain of verbal abuse and shows how the resulting confusion disempowers women who are battered.

Bolles, Richard N. *The Three Boxes of Life and How to Get Out of Them: An Introduction to Life/Work Planning.* Berkeley, Calif.: Ten Speed Press, 1978. A comprehensive guide to planning and managing your life in the areas of education, work, and retirement. This book is filled with insight and information directed toward finding out about the world and your place in it.

—. *The 1990 What Color Is Your Parachute?: A Practical Manual for Job-Hunters & Career Changers.* Berkeley, Calif.: Ten Speed Press. If you are looking for a career, want to move ahead in your career, or just want to be able to better assess your abilities and skills, this book is a must. It is updated and published annually.

Bridges, William. *Transitions: Making Sense of Life's Changes.* Reading, Mass.: Addison-Wesley Publishing Company, Inc., 1986. Life is change. However, major changes and sudden changes can be very difficult. William Bridges shows us what to expect and how to cope.

Jeffers, Susan. *Feel the Fear and Do It Anyway.* New York: Ballantine Books, 1987. If you take the steps Susan Jeffers recommends, you are sure to grow in confidence and self-esteem. If you want to take action in your life, this book is a must.

Kaschak, Ellyn. *Engendered Lives: A New Psychology of Women's Experience.* New York: Basic Books, 1992. This in-depth book explores how women's identity is shaped by the values and expectations of the dominant male culture.

Keirsey, David, and Marilyn Bates. *Please Understand Me: Character and Temperament Types.* Del Mar, Calif.: Prometheus Nemesis Book Co., 1984. After you score your answer sheet in this book, you may find your type of temperament and can read all about yourself.

Lindbergh, Anne Morrow. *Gift from the Sea*. New York: Vintage Books, 1978. A little book of wisdom about finding your center and understanding yourself.

McCullough, Christopher J. *Nobody's Victim: Freedom from Therapy and Recovery*. New York: Clarkson Potter, 1995. Interesting and insightful, this book inspires readers to go beyond therapy and recovery to create fulfilling and meaningful lives.

Ross, Ruth. *Prospering Woman: A Complete Guide to Achieving the Full, Abundant Life*. Mill Valley, CA: Whatever Publishing, Inc., 1982. If you seek financial stability and want to raise your self-esteem, this book shows you how.

Sher, Barbara, with Annie Gottlieb. *Wishcraft: How to Get What You Really Want*. New York: Ballantine Books, 1979. This entertaining and encouraging book takes you through imaginary journeys where you discover your strengths and talents. You also find out how to meet your goals, build confidence, and gain support.

Sinetar, Marsha. *Do What You Love, The Money Will Follow: Discovering Your Right Livelihood*. New Jersey: Paulist Press, 1987. This book reveals the inner rewards (high self-esteem) and outer rewards (money) of integrating who we are with our own life's work. This book is truly a guide to authentic living.

—. *Elegant Choices, Healing Choices*. New Jersey: Paulist Press, 1988. A nurturing and inspiring book that presents a way of recognizing the many choices we have in our everyday lives to create the best for ourselves. I highly recommend this book.

Stoddard, Alexandra. *Living A Beautiful Life*. New York: Random House, Inc., 1986. No detail is too small when it comes to creating a beautiful and nurturing environment for yourself. From simple to elaborate, there is an idea for you. This book says you are worth it.

BOOKS ABOUT THERAPY

Following are some additional books that discuss therapy from a systemic or narrative approach. I recommend them to therapists and to any reader seeking more information.

Anderson, W.T. *Reality Isn't What It Used To Be*. San Francisco: Harper, 1990.

Bateson, G. *Steps to an Ecology of Mind*. New York: Chandler, 1972.

Berger, P.L., and T. Luckmann. *The Social Construction of Reality*. New York: Anchor Books, 1967.

Epston, D., and M. White. *Experience, Contradiction, Narrative and Imagination: Selected Papers of David Epston and Michael White*. Adelaide, South Australia: Dulwich Centre Publications, 1992.

Friedman, S., editor. *The New Language of Change: Constructive Collaboration in Psychotherapy.* New York: W.W. Norton, 1993.

Gergen, K. *The Saturated Self: Dilemmas of Identity in Contemporary Life.* New York: Basic Books, 1991.

Gilligan, S. and R. Price, editors. *Therapeutic Conversations.* New York: W.W. Norton, 1993.

Griffith, J.L., and M.C. Griffith. *The Body Speaks: Therapeutic Dialogues for Mind-Body Problems.* New York: Basic Books, 1994.

McNamee, S. and K. Gergen. *Therapy as Social Construction.* Newbury Park, Calif.: Sage Publications, 1992.

Parry, A. and R.E. Doan. *Story Revision: Narrative Therapy in the Post Modern World.* New York: Guilford, 1994.

White, Michael. *Selected Papers.* Adelaide, South Australia: Dulwich Centre Publications, 1989.

White, M. and D. Epston. *Narrative Means to Therapeutic Ends.* New York: W.W. Norton, 1990.

Books published by Dulwich Centre Publications can be ordered from their North American distributor: Dulwich Centre Publications, P.O. Box 34185, station D, Vancouver, B.C., Canada. V6J 4N1; phone/fax (604) 688-7865.

Survey

I invite you, the reader, to answer the following questionnaire so that we might know more about verbal abuse in relationships. Your participation in this survey will be of value and is greatly appreciated. You do not in any way need to reveal your identity.

Please check the applicable response and add any additional notes you feel are appropriate. Return to:

Patricia Evans
Evans Interpersonal Communications Institute
P.O. Box 589
Alamo, CA 94507
Phone (925) 934-5972; Fax (925) 933-9636
E-mail EVANSbooks@aol.com
Web site: www.PatriciaEvans.com
Web site: www.VerbalAbuse.com

Please include a self-addressed stamped envelope if you need a reply by mail. Return calls outside of the 925 and 415 area codes will be placed collect.

I thank you in advance.

SURVEY

I am   ❏ female   ❏ male

I am   ❏ married   ❏ single

I am   ❏ under 25   ❏ under 35   ❏ under 55   ❏ 55 or over

My relationship is (was)   ❏ heterosexual   ❏ homosexual

I am (was) in my relationship

    ❏ 1–3 years

    ❏ 4–10 years

    ❏ 11–20 years

    ❏ more than 20 years

I experienced verbal abuse quite often

    ❏ in my relationship

    ❏ in childhood

    ❏ from my father

    ❏ from my mother

    ❏ from other caretakers

    ❏ from family friends

    ❏ from relatives

    ❏ from co-workers

    ❏ from bosses

    ❏ from adult children

    ❏ from teachers

    ❏ from kids at school

    ❏ other _____

_____

I am in a verbally abusive relationship now.   ❏ Yes   ❏ No

(If you answered "yes" to the above question, please answer the following 5 questions.)

I feel unable to leave the abusive relationship.   ❏ Yes   ❏ No

I feel trapped.   ❏ Yes   ❏ No

Even though I am abused, I feel I love my mate.   ❏ Yes   ❏ No

I believe my mate will change.   ❏ Yes   ❏ No

It has never occurred to me to leave.   ❏ Yes   ❏ No

Other _____

_____

I am (was) in a verbally abusive relationship.   ❏ Yes   ❏ No

(If you answered "yes" please answer the next question.)

Did the frequency and intensity of the abusive incidents increase over time?   ❏ Yes   ❏ No

In my adult life, I have never been in a verbally abusive relationship.
❏ Yes   ❏ No

I believe that I may
    ❏ often
    ❏ occasionally
    ❏ rarely be verbally abusive toward others.

I have been hit, pushed or shoved by my mate.   ❏ Yes   ❏ No
My mate has threatened to hit me.   ❏ Yes   ❏ No
At times I am afraid of my mate.   ❏ Yes   ❏ No
I think verbal abuse has affected my self-esteem, confidence and
happiness in a negative way.
    ❏ not at all
    ❏ somewhat
    ❏ very much
    ❏ doesn't apply because I've never been verbally abused.

I have *most often* been verbally abused in the following ways (please
check 5 or fewer categories of verbal abuse).
    ❏ 1. Withholding
    ❏ 2. Countering
    ❏ 3. Discounting
    ❏ 4. Abusive jokes
    ❏ 5. Blocking/diverting
    ❏ 6. Accusing/blaming
    ❏ 7. Judging/criticizing
    ❏ 8. Trivializing
    ❏ 9. Undermining
    ❏ 10. Threatening
    ❏ 11. Name calling
    ❏ 12. Ordering
    ❏ 13. Forgetting
    ❏ 14. Denial
    ❏ 15. Abusive anger

When I was verbally abused I usually:
- ❑ Thought I had said or done something wrong.
- ❑ Felt confused and unsure.
- ❑ Felt sad and/or hurt.
- ❑ Felt stunned or shocked.
- ❑ Thought there was something I was missing.
- ❑ Thought the abuser didn't understand something.
- ❑ Other: _____

_____

_____

After reading this book I:
- ❑ Better understand what verbal abuse is.
- ❑ Am more confused than ever about verbal abuse.
- ❑ Am more able to respond appropriately to verbal abuse.

I would like to know more about: _____

_____

In order to deal with verbal abuse now I need to:
- ❑ Be more alert to it.
- ❑ Be less afraid of the abuser.
- ❑ Be more financially secure.
- ❑ Be more confident.
- ❑ Have more support from family, co-workers and friends.
- ❑ Other: _____

_____

_____

Index

Verbal Abuse
Survivors Speak Out
On Relationship and Recovery

Verbal Abuse Survivors Speak Out draws upon the experience of thousands who responded to Patricia Evans' first book, *The Verbally Abusive Relationship*. Their letters highlight Evans' in-depth exploration of verbal abuse issues and bring increasing clarity and insight to the reader. You will learn the stories of other women who have struggled against the fear and oppression engendered by verbal abuse, and have made the decision to insist on a change. Some of these women are just beginning to understand the problem, some are planning to leave their relationships, some have already left, and some, with their spouse, have made a commitment to change their relationship for the better. Their stories can give validation to suspicions and fears, and can provide courage, hope, and a road map for healing and recovery.

Trade paperback, 5½" x 8½", 224 pages, $14.95
ISBN: 1-55850-304-8

Available wherever books are sold.
For more information, or to order, call 800-258-0929
or visit *www.adamsmedia.com*
Adams Media, 57 Littlefield Street, Avon, MA 02322

Controlling People

How to Recognize, Understand, and Deal with People Who Try to Control You

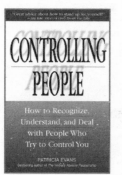

Does this sound like someone you know?

- Always needs to be right
- Tells you who you are and what you think
- Feels attacked when questioned
- Is threatened by people who are "different"

If any one of the above traits sounds familiar, help is on the way! In *Controlling People*, Patricia Evans tackles the "controlling personality," and reveals how and why these people try to run other people's lives. *Controlling People* helps you unravel the senseless behavior that plagues both the controller and the victim. Can the pattern, or spell, be broken? Yes!

By understanding the compelling forces involved, you can be a catalyst for change and actually become a spell-breaker. Once the spell is broken and the controller sees other as they really are, a genuine connection can be forged and healing can occur. *Controlling People* gives you the wisdom, power, and comfort you need to be a stronger, happier, and more independent person.

Trade paperback, 5½" x 8½", 320 pages, $14.95
ISBN: 1-58062-569-X

Available wherever books are sold.
For more information, or to order, call 800-258-0929
or visit *www.adamsmedia.com*
Adams Media, 57 Littlefield Street, Avon, MA 02322